EMANUEL SWEDI

JOURNAL OF DREAMS
AND
SPIRITUAL EXPERIENCES

TRANSLATED FROM THE SWEDISH BY

REV. C. TH. ODHNER

INTRODUCTION

Emanuel Swedenborg, at various periods of his life, was in the habit of keeping a diary. The most extensive and best known of his diaries is the Spiritual Diary, in which, from the year 1747 to 1765, he made notes of his experiences in the spiritual world.

As far as is known, Swedenborg did not begin to keep a diary until the year 1733, when he wrote down a very brief sketch of his first two foreign journeys, beginning with the year 1710. This was followed by a larger itinerary, describing his travels in Germany during the years 1733 and 1734, but it was discontinued during the year 1735, when Swedenborg remained at his home in Stockholm. When, in the year 1736, he started on his fourth and most extensive foreign journey, he again began to keep an itinerary, or, more properly speaking, a diary, which he kept up until March. 1739, describing his travels in Holland, Flanders, France, and Italy. It has been reported that Swedenborg, in the manuscript containing this Diary, also described some remarkable dreams which he experienced during these years, but that his heirs removed the pages containing these dreams. Only two leaves, however, are missing from this manuscript. (Doc. 11:130.)

We come now to Swedenborg's third attempt at keeping a diary,—the manuscript which has become known as "SWEDENBORG'S DREAMS, 1744,"—an octavo pocket book, (6½ by 4 inches), bound in parchment and containing 104 written pages. Of the history of this Codex nothing is known except the fact that it was found by Mr. L. B. Borberg in the library of the late R. Scheringson, professor and lector in the city of Westeras, who died in 1849 at the age of ninety years. Concerning this Professor Scheringson nothing further was known until we found that he was one of the earliest opponents of the New Church, having published at Upsala, in the year 1787, a work in two volumes, entitled DISSERTATIO SISTENS OBSERVATIONES NONNULLAS DE PHILOSOPHIA RECENTIORUM PLATONICORUM, INDOLEM ATQUE ORIGINEM FANATISMI NOSTRI ÆVI

ILLUSTRANTES, (A Dissertation presenting certain observations concerning the philosophy of the Neo-Platonists, illustrating the genius and origin of the Fanaticism of the present age). According to Professor Sundelin, in his HISTORY OF SWEDENBORGIANISM IN SWEDEN, (p. 245), this work was an insidious and learned attack upon the theology of the New Church, attempting to prove that Swedenborg had borrowed almost the whole of his system from the Neo-Platonic philosophers.

But how did it come about that the manuscript of Swedenborg's DREAMS was found in the library of this enemy of Swedenborg? We do not know, but the fact that Bishop Lars Benzelstjerna, who was Swedenborg's nephew and, therefore, one of his heirs, was Bishop of the Diocese of Westeras, suggests the probability that he had obtained possession of the manuscript in question, and had loaned it to Professor Scheringson, with whom it had remained, forgotten, more than half a century.

In the year 1858 the existence of this manuscript became known to Gustaf E. Klemming, the chief librarian of the Royal Library in Stockholm, and it was now purchased by this institution. Klemming was an avowed enemy of the New Church, but was deeply interested in Swedenborgianism as a curious literary phenomenon, and he made a specialty of collecting all works relating to it. The little pocket-book, which in many places was extremely difficult to decipher, was now placed in the hands of Mr. F. A. Dahlgren, amanuensis at the National Archives, and this expert chirographist produced a clean copy, which, in 1859, was published in an edition of 99 numbered copies by P. A. Nordstedt and Sons, Royal Printers at Stockholm, under the title: SWEDENBORGS DROMMAR. (SWEDENBORG'S DREAMS, 1744, TOGETHER WITH SOME OTHER NOTES BY HIM. FROM THE ORIGINAL MANUSCRIPTS.)

As was expected, the publication of the Drommar created a tremendous sensation both within and without the New Church. Soon after the appearance of the volume, a review, not of a friendly character, and undoubtedly written by Dr. Klemming, was published in the AFTONBLADET, the leading evening paper of Stockholm.

The few and scattered New Church people in Sweden, usually very timid, now took courage, and, in the year 1860, issued a second Swedish edition of the work, prefaced by twenty-four pages of "REFLECTIONS ON THE LATELY DISCOVERED DREAMS OF SWEDENBORG." (Stockholm, J. and A. Riis.) This unsigned preface was written by Lady Anna Fredrika Ehrenborg, a noble, gifted, and fearless authoress, who had championed the cause of the New Church in many publications and had edited two distinctive New Church journals, NAGOT NYTT, (Something New), and ETT CHRISTLIGT SANDEBUD, (A Christian Messenger). In her "Reflections," Lady Ehrenborg explained the real nature of these "Dreams" of Swedenborg, describing the transition state through which Swedenborg was passing in the year 1744, and the spiritual temptations and vastations he was then sustaining.

Dr. Wilkinson, in 1860, completed a first English translation of the Dreams; it was never published, but the manuscript is still preserved in the library of the Swedenborg Society in London.

During the next two years there appeared what was claimed to be a new and independent English version, but which was in reality nothing but a clumsily disguised transcription of Dr. Wilkinson's translation. Mr. William White, in his second, (and hostile), Biography of Swedenborg, (1867-1868), asserts that "Baron Constant Dirckinck Holmfeld, of Copenhagen, has very kindly made for me a translation into English of the rough and difficult Swedish of 'the DREAMS.' This translation, with some omissions, was printed in THE DAWN for 1861-62, a monthly magazine published by Mr. F. Pitman. 20 Paternosterrow, London. For the help of the curious American readers I may mention that THE CRISIS, a paper published at La Porte, Indiana, reprinted in its columns 'THE DREAMS,' as they appeared in THE DAWN." (Vol. 1. p. 197.) Dr. R. L. Tafel, in his DOCUMENTS CONCERNING SWEDENBORG, has thoroughly exposed the fraudulent character of the version published in THE DAWN, (Doc. II. p. 1312.)

It was not until 1877 that the English-speaking New Church public became more generally acquainted with Swedenborg's "Dreams," and then only through the incomplete translation made by Dr. R. L. Tafel, and published in the second volume of his DOCUMENTS.

In our new translation we have introduced a new numbering of the paragraphs, as we cannot follow Dr. Tafel's numbering on account of his unnumbered omissions. The passages which he omitted we have turned into Latin, as the students of the Church certainly should have an opportunity to judge of their character and contents. Sentences which seem unintelligible in the original we have simply translated word for word, hoping that some day a phototyped copy of the original text will clear up some of the obscure places. The Italics in the text represent words and lines underscored by Swedenborg.

The contents of the manuscript may be described briefly as follows:

1. A meager account of Swedenborg's fifth foreign journey,—leaving Stockholm on July 21st, 1743, arriving at Stralsund, Aug. 6th, passing on through Wismar, Hamburg, Bremen and

Gröningen, to Harlingen in Holland, where he arrived on Aug. 20th, on his way to The Hague. Here the itinerary abruptly ends, for two leaves have been torn out of the MS., and these are followed by 16 blank pages.

2. Then come two written pages containing eleven numbered annotations, briefly recording some undated dreams, with observations as to the mental state of the writer after his arrival at The Hague.

3. The body of the Journal itself, dated from March 24th to October 27th, 1744, covering eighty-nine pages of the written MS. From these we learn that Swedenborg remained at The Hague until April 22d. On April 23d he was in Leyden, on April 24th in Amsterdam, returning to The Hague the next day. On May 4th he arrived at Harwick, England, and was in London on May 5th.

4. After an interval of sixteen blank pages there follow, on p. 101, a few additional notes concerning some dreams, and then again two blank pages.

5. Some memoranda concerning transactions with his bankers in Holland and England, on p.

104, the latest date recorded being Dec. 21st, 1744. This, again, is followed by two blank pages.

6. Finally, on p. 108, an undated Latin note concerning Verities being represented by virtuous ladies, and concerning himself as their humble servant The style of the writing, both as to chirography and orthography, is that of a man getting out of his bed at almost any hour of the night in order to jot down his dreams, immediately upon becoming awake or half-awake. A man in such a state would naturally pay no attention, whatsoever, to finish of style, correct spelling, or punctuation, but no one can blame the writer, under the conditions, and inasmuch as he did not write for the benefit of anyone but himself.

C. TH. ODHNER.

Emanuel Swedenborg's Journal of Dreams

1743-1744

[1] 1743. July 21. I started on my journey from Stockholm, and arrived at Ystad on the 27th, having passed through the cities of [Söder]talje, Nyköping, Norrköping, Linköping, Grenna and Jönköping. At Ystad I met the Countess de la Gardie with her two young ladies and two [young] counts; also Count Fersen, Major Lantingshausen and Magister Klingenberg. On July 31st General Stenflycht arrived with his son, and Captain Schächta.

[2] On account of contrary winds we were not able to sail until August 5th. I travelled in company with General Stenflycht. On August 6th we arrived at Stralsund, and early on the 7th we entered the city. The Countess and the General left the same day.

[3] In Stralsund I viewed again the fortress from the Badenthor even to the Franken, Triebseer and Knieperthor; I saw also the houses where king Charles XII. had lodged, the Meierfeld palace, and the churches of St. Nicholas, St. James (which was ruined during the siege), and St. Mary. I visited Colonel Schwerin, the Commandant, the Superintendent Loper, and the Postmaster Crivits. In the Church of St. Nicholas I was shown a clock that had been struck by lightning in the years 1670, 1683. 1688, just as the hand pointed to 6 o'clock. Afterwards I viewed the new fortifications outside the Knieperthor. I also met Carl Jesper Benzelius; examined the water works which supply the city, they consist of two Archimedean screws, [*slangangar*]

[4] On August 9th I left Stralsund, passing through Dammgarten. In the Mecklenburg territory I passed by Ribnitz to Rostock, where I viewed eight churches, five large ones and three smaller ones, and a convent for women; there were eight of them, but they were in freedom.

[5] Thence I travelled to Wismar, where there are six churches; the best of them are St. Mary's and St. George's.

On [August] 11th I left Wismar. On the way I visited Gadebusch, where was the battle between the Swedes and the Danes; then I came to Ratzeburg, which is surrounded by a swamp, on account of which we passed over a long bridge.

[6] On [August] 12th I arrived at Hamburg and took lodgings at the Kaisershof, where al so the Countess De la Gardie was staying. I met Baron Hamilton, Reuterholm, Trievald, König, Assessor Awerman, and was introduced to Prince Augustus, the brother of his royal Highness, who spoke Swedish. Afterwards I was introduced by the marshal-in-chief, Lesch, to his royal Highness, Adolphus Frederic, to whom I submitted the contents [of my book] which is to be printed, and showed him the reviews of the preceding work.

[7] On [August] 17th I left Hamburg, across the Elbe to Buxtehude, where, to the extent of a [German] mile, I viewed the most charming country I have yet seen in Germany; we passed

through a continuous orchard of apple trees, pear trees, plums, walnuts, and chestnut trees, and also linden and elms.

[8] On [August] 18th I arrived at Bremen, which has good ramparts and suburbs; the best is Neustadt. Near the bridge leading to it there are eleven river mills close to one another. I viewed the Town Hall in the market place, and the great Roland [statue], which is the sign of a free city; afterwards I viewed the Church of St. Nicholas, the Cathedral, and the hospital. There are also some statues in the town.

[9] On [August] 20th I travelled from Bremen to Leer, passing through Oldenburg, which is a county belonging to the king of Denmark. [Leer] has good ramparts, with plenty of water round about. I likewise passed through Neuschanz. Near Leer there is a fortification called Leerort, belonging to Holland. I journeyed thence to Gröningen, which is a large city under the Prince of Orange. At Leeuwarden I saw his palace, and also the palace of his mother, which is called the

Princess' palace; likewise the Town Hall, etc. We arrived there by canal boat.

[10] From Gröningen there are two ways, one by Harlingen, and the other by Lemmer: the former is reached by canal boat, the latter by carriage: but we chose the road to Harlingen through Leeuwarden.

From Harlingen, which is a large town,

[Here the manuscript abruptly breaks off. The Swedish editor of the original manuscript adds in a note: "The continuation is missing. It is impossible to decide whether it was written or not, for the word 'stad' [town] is at the end of page 6: this is followed by several blank pages; but it is probable that some (4?) pages have been torn out. On the strips remaining from leaves that have been cut out, there are seen some large numerals written by an unskilled hand, perhaps that of a child."

The manuscript then continues as follows:

[11] 1. In [my] youth and the Gustavian family.

2. In Venice, about the beautiful palace.

3. In Sweden, about the white cloud of the sky.

4. In Leipzig, about the one who lay in seething water.

5. About the one who tumbled with the chain into the depth.

6. About the king who gave something very precious in a peasant's hut.

7. About the man-servant who wished that I would go away on a journey.

[12] 8. About my joys at night.

—I wondered at myself that there remained nothing of [the desire] to work for my own glory, so as to have sensation thereof.

—that I was not inclined towards the sex, as I had been in all my days.

9. How I have been in wakeful ecstasies almost the whole time.

[13] 10. How I opposed myself to the spirit.

—and how I then liked it, but afterwards found it to have been foolish things, without life and coherence.

—and that consequently a mass of what I have written must be [such], since I have not in that degree forsaken the power of the spirit, wherefore the faults are all my own, but the verities not my own.

—indeed, I sometimes fell into impatience and thoughts, that I wished to make insistent demands, when there was not the easy progress that I wanted, since I did not labor for my own sake; I found my unworthiness less, and gave thanks for the grace.

[14] 11. How, after arriving at The Hague, I found that the impulse and self-love for my work had passed away, at which I wondered.

—how the inclination for women, which had been my chief passion, so suddenly ceased.

—how during the whole time I had enjoyed the best of sleep at night, which has been more than delightful.

—how my ecstasies before and after sleep.

—my clear thoughts in the matters.

[15] How I had resisted the power of the Holy Spirit, and what then happened; how I beheld

hideous spectres, without life, horribly involved, and within [something] moved itself; with a beast which attacked me but not the child.

[16] I seemed to be reclining on a mountain beneath which there was an abyss; there were projections; I was lying there, trying to get up, holding on to a projection, without foot-hold, an abyss beneath: it signifies that I wished to rescue myself from the abyss by my own power, which was not possible.

[17] How a woman was by my side, just as if I had been awake; I wanted to know who she was. She spoke in a low voice, but said that she was pure, but that I had a bad odor. She was, as I believe, my guardian angel, for the temptation then began.

1744. March 24-25.

[18] 1. I was standing by a machine which was moved by a wheel; its spokes involved me more and more and carried me up so that I could not escape: I awoke. [It signifies] either that I need to be kept further in the dilemma, or else that it

concerned the lungs in the womb, on which subject I then wrote immediately afterwards; both.

[19] 2. I was in a garden containing many fine beds, one of which I desired to own, but I looked about to see if there was any road to walk out; I also seemed to see it, and thought of another: there was one there who was picking away a heap of invisible vermin and killed them; he said they were bedbugs which some person had carried thither and thrown in, infesting those who were there. I did not see them, but some other little insect, which I dropped on a white linen cloth beside a woman: it was the impurity which ought to be rooted out of me.

[20] 3. Quite freely and boldly I stepped down a large stairway; by and by there was a ladder, below it there was a hole which went down to quite a great depth; it was difficult to get to the other side without falling into the hole. On the other side there were persons to whom I reached out my hand to help them cross over, I awoke. It is the danger in which I am of falling into the abyss, unless I receive help.

[21] 4. I spoke long and familiarly with our Successor in Sweden, who changed into a woman. Afterwards I spoke with Carl Broman, [saying] that he ought to be in favor of him; he answered something; [then I spoke] with Erland Broman, [saying] that I had returned here. I do not know what this means, unless it has to do with what follows.

[22] 5. I came into a magnificent chamber and spoke with a woman who was governess of the court. She wished to relate something to me; then came the queen and passed through to another chamber; it seemed to be the same one who represented our Successor. I went out for I was rather meanly dressed, as I had just returned from my journey, [wearing] a long old overcoat, and without hat and wig; I wondered that she condescended to come to me; she related that a certain one had given all the jewels to his mistress, but he had received them back again in this manner that it was told her that he had not given her the best, whereupon she threw away the jewels.

[23] She asked me to come again, but I excused myself on the plea that I was so shabbily dressed and had no wig, and must go home first; she said it did not matter. This has reference to that which I was then about to write and begin the Epilogue of the second part, to which I wanted to write a preface, but there is no need of it. I acted accordingly. What she told about the jewels had reference to the truths which are discovered to a person, but are taken away again, because she was offended that she had not received all. I afterwards saw the jewels in [my?] hands and a great ruby in the middle.

[March] 25-26

[24] It seemed as if I took a key and went in; the doorkeeper examined the keys which I had; I showed them all, in case I should have two, but it seemed that Hesselius had another. I was arrested and put under guard; there came to me many in carriages. It seemed to me I had done nothing wrong, but I remembered that it might be considered in a bad light if it turns out that I had

taken the key. I awoke. There may be various interpretations, as that I have taken the key to anatomy, while the other one which Hesselius had, was the key to medicine; as also that the key to the lungs is the pulmonary artery, and thus to all the motions of the body; or [it may be interpreted] spiritually.

[25] I asked to be cured of my illness; there was given me a heap of rags to buy for [it]; I took half of them, and looked out for the other half, but returned all the rags. He said that he himself would buy [something] that would lead to a cure. The rags were my corporeal thoughts by which I wished to cure myself, but they were good for nothing.

[26] Afterwards I went out and saw many black images; a black one was thrown to me; I saw that he could not get about with his foot; I believe it meant that natural reason cannot agree with spiritual reason.

[March] 30-31.

[27] I saw a group of women, one who wrote a letter; I took it but do not know what became of it. She was sewing, and a yellow man struck her on the back; wished she should get more blows, but it was enough; this, I believe, concerns what I am writing and have written,—our philosophy.

[28] I saw a very handsome woman by a window where a child was placing roses; she took me by the hand and conducted me; it signifies what I am writing, and my suffering, which should lead me, as I believe.

[29] I saw a magnificent procession of men, adorned so handsomely that I have never seen anything more handsome, but it soon disappeared. It was, as I believe, experimental science which now is greatly in fashion.

April 1-2.

[30] I rode in the air on a horse; went into all the rooms, the kitchen, and other places, hunting for one whom I did not find; the rooms were untidy; finally I was carried through the air into a

drawing room where I received two beautiful loaves of bread, and then I found him again. Quite a number of people were there and the room was in good order. Signifies the Lord's Supper.

[31] King Charles was sitting in a dark room and said something, but somewhat indistinctly; afterwards one at the table inquired whether he had not received the information he had asked about; he replied. Yes. He afterwards closed the windows, and I helped him with the curtains. Afterwards I mounted a horse, but did not take the road I had intended but went across hills and mountains, riding swiftly. A wagon with a load followed after me, and I could not get away from it; still the horse by the load became tired, and [the driver] wanted to get him into some place; he came in, and the horse became like a slaughtered, bloody beast, fallen down. It signifies that I have received all that I have thought for my instruction, and that I am perhaps taking a wrong road; the load was my remaining work, which followed me, who on that road became so tired and dead.

[32] I stepped out of a carriage; it was driven into a lake. While driving into it the coachman cried to the other carriage to take care, as there was danger when he drove in; I looked at the other carriage; behind it there seemed to be a screen which was unfolded like an umbrella. I, together with the man who sat behind, took the screen, went in, and folded it together. It meant that the beginning of my work was difficult; the other carriage was warned to look out, and that I ought to draw in my sails and not make the notes so long.

[April] 2-3.

[33] Two persons came; they entered a house which, though built, was not yet furnished; they went about but did not seem favorable: we realized that our power was gone, and were afraid of them. One of them came to me and said that they intended to inflict a punishment on me the next Thursday before Easter, unless I made my escape. I did not know how to get out, but he told me he would show me the way. I awoke. It means that I,

in an unprepared and untidy hut, had invited the highest beings to visit me, and that they had found it untidy and that I ought to be punished, but I was most graciously shown the way by which to avoid their wrath.

[34] There was a beggar who cried that he wanted some pork; they wished to give him something else, but he insistently called for pork. I awoke. It has the same significance, I believe.

[35] I saw two groups of soldiers, dressed in blue, who marched in two troops past my window which stood ajar. I desired to look out and watch the marching of the first troop, which seemed to me magnificent. I awoke. It means a gracious guard, that I may not perish.

N. B.—3-4 April, 1744, which was the day before Easter.

[36] I experienced nothing the whole night, although I repeatedly woke up; I thought everything was past and gone, and that I was forsaken or driven away. Towards the morning it seemed to me I was riding, and the direction was shown to me, but when I looked it was dark, and I

found I had lost my way on account of the darkness. But then it lightened up and I saw that I had gone wrong; I saw the road and the forests and groves to which I should travel, and behind them the sky. I awoke. There came then a thought, as it were spontaneous, about the first life, and, in consequence, about the other life, and it seemed to me everything was full of grace. I fell a-weeping because I had not been loving but rather had offended Him who has led me and shown me the way even unto the kingdom of grace, and that I, unworthy one, have been received into grace.

[April] 4-5. I went to God's table.

[37] It was said that one more courier had arrived; I said that this probably means that [rest of the sentence is obliterated].

There was sung the melody and a line which I remember from the hymn "Jesus is my friend, the best one."

It seemed to me that green buds had opened.

[April] 5-6.

[38] Master day was on April 5th, when I went to God's table. The temptation still continued, mostly in the afternoon until six o'clock, still nothing definite. It was an anxiety as ii I were damned and in hell, yet always the hope which the Holy Spirit granted, according to Paul's Epistle to the Romans, V:5, remained strong throughout. The evil one had power given him to disturb my inmost by various thoughts.

[39] On Easter day, after the communion, I was inwardly content, but still outwardly sad. The temptation came in the afternoon, in an entirely different manner, but strongly, for I was assured that my sins were forgiven, but still I could not govern my fugitive thoughts so as to restrain some expressions opposed to my better knowledge; it was from the evil one, by permission. Prayer gave some relief, and also the Word of God; the faith was present entirely, but the confidence and love seemed to be absent.

[40] I went to bed at 9 o'clock; the temptation, accompanied with trembling, continued until half-

past ten. I then fell into a sleep in which my whole temptation was represented to me: how Er[land] B[roman] sought by various means to get me on his side, so as to be of that party, (voluptuousness, riches, vanity), but he could not gain me over. I became still more obstinate against him because he showed contempt. [41] Afterwards I was together with a crouching dark-grey snake, and it was B[roman's] dog. I struck at him many times with a club but tried in vain to hit him on the head; he wanted to bite me but could not; I seized him by the throat, and he could not bite me, nor was I able to do him much harm; finally I got hold of him by the jaws and squeezed him hard, and also by the nose which I squeezed so that the venom burst forth. I said that while the dog did not belong to me, still, as he wanted to bite me, I had to chastise him. Thereupon it seemed someone said he had not gotten me to say one word to him, and then I quarreled with him. When 1 awoke, the words which I said were: Shut your mouth!

[42] From this, without further interpretation, may be seen the nature of the temptation, but on

the other hand how great has been the grace of God, through the merit of Christ, and the operation of the Holy Spirit, to whom be glory from eternity to eternity. The thought at once occurred to me, how great is the grace of the Lord, which accounts to us that we have resisted in temptation, and which is imputed to us, when nevertheless it is nothing but the grace and operation of God, being His and not our own, and He overlooks the weaknesses that we have shown in it, which have been manifold; and also how great a glory our Lord bestows after a little time of tribulation.

[43] Afterwards I fell asleep, and it seemed the whole night how in various ways I was first joined with others, by what was sinful; and then how I was enveloped, by wonderful and indescribable circumvolutions, so that during the whole night I was inaugurated in a wonderful manner, and then it was said: "Is there any Jacobite more than honest?" Then, in conclusion. I was received with an embrace. Afterwards it was said that "he ought not to be thus called or thus named," but how, I do

not remember, if it was not Jacobite, this I cannot describe; it was a mystical series.

[44] Afterwards I awoke and fell asleep again a number of times, and all [that I dreamed] was in answer to my thoughts, yet in such a manner that there was such a life and such a glory in the whole of it that I cannot describe the least particular, for all of it was heavenly. At the time it was clear to me, but after it I cannot express anything. In short, I was in heaven and heard a speech which no human tongue can utter wath the life that is there or the glory and inmost delight that flow from it.

Except for this I was awake, as in a heavenly ecstasy, which is also indescribable.

[45] At nine o'clock I went to bed and arose between nine and ten, having been in bed from twelve to thirteen hours. To the Highest be praise, honor and glory! Hallowed be His name! Holy, holy, Lord God Zebaoth!

[46] How by experience I learned what it means not to love angels more than God, as this had nearly overthrown the whole work. In comparison

with our Lord no respect must be paid to them, but only in respect to their assistance, since [their] love is far inferior.

[47] I found in me as it were a radiance, that the greatest happiness would be to become a martyr, for the consideration of the indescribable grace, combined with the love towards God, makes one desire to sustain that torture which is nothing compared with the eternal torment, and the least thing would be to sacrifice one's life.

[48] I had also in my mind and in my body as it were a sensation of an indescribable delight, so that if it had been more intense, the body would have been as it were dissolved from the delight alone.

This took place in the night between the first and second day after Easter, and during the whole of the latter day.

6-7 April N. B. N. B. N. B.

[49] In the evening I came into another sort of temptation, as follows: Between eight and nine in the evening, while T was reading concerning the

miracles of God wrought through Moses, it seemed to me as if something of my own understanding mixed itself into it, so that I was not able to have the strong faith that I ought to have. I believed and yet did not believe. I was thinking that on this account the angels and God revealed themselves to shepherds and not to the philosopher who allows his understanding to take part in the play, as is always the way when, for instance, a person asks why God made use of the wind when He collected the locusts; why He hardened Pharaoh's heart; why He did not work immediately, and other such things at which indeed I smiled mentally, but which nevertheless caused the faith to be less firm. [50] I looked at the fire [in my stove] and said to myself. Neither ought I to believe that the fire exists, when nevertheless the external senses are more fallacious than what God says, who is Truth itself; I ought to believe it rather than myself. In such and other thoughts I spent an hour or an hour and a half, and smiled in my mind at the tempter. It is to be noted that during the same day I had travelled to Delft, and the whole day I had been graciously permitted to be in profound spiritual thoughts, as profound and beautiful as I had ever experienced, and this during the entire day, which was the work of the Spirit, whom I found to be with me.

[51] At ten o'clock I went to bed and felt somewhat better. Half an hour afterwards I heard a noise beneath my head and I then thought that the tempter had departed. Immediately there came over me a powerful tremor, from the head and over the whole body, together with a resounding noise, and this occurred a number of times. I found that something holy had encompassed me. [52] I then fell asleep, but about twelve, one, or two o'clock in the night there came over me a very powerful tremor from the head to the feet, accompanied with a booming sound as if many winds had clashed against one another. It was indescribable, and it shook me and prostrated me on my face. In the moment that I was prostrated I became wide awake, and I saw that I had been thrown down. [53] I wondered what it meant, and I spoke as if I were awake, but still I

found that the words were put into my mouth, and I said, "Oh, Thou Almighty Jesus Christ, who of Thy great mercy deignest to come to so great a sinner, make me worthy of this grace!" I kept my hands folded and I prayed, and then there came forth a hand which strongly pressed my hands. [54] I then continued my prayer, saying, "Thou hast promised to receive in grace all sinners; Thou canst not otherwise than keep Thy words!" In the same moment I was sitting at His bosom and beheld Him face to face. It was a countenance of a holy mien, and all was such that it cannot be expressed, and also smiling, so that I believe that His countenance was such also while He lived [in the world]. He spoke to me and asked if I had a bill of health, [*om jag har sundhets pass.*] I answered, "Lord, Thou knowest better than I." He said, "Well, then do," [*Na sa gior*]. This I found in my mind to signify, "Love me truly," or "Do what thou hast promised." O God, impart to me grace for this! I found it was not in my own power. I awoke, with tremors. [55] I then again came into such a state that in my thoughts I was neither sleeping nor awake. I thought. What may this be? Is it Christ, the Son of God, that I have seen? It is a sin that I am doubting it, but as it is commanded that we are to try the spirits, I reflected on everything, and I found from that which had occurred the previous night, that I had been purified by the Holy Spirit during the whole night, and encompassed and preserved, and thus prepared for this purpose. And from the fact that I fell upon my face,—and that the words which I spoke and the prayer which I said did not come from myself, but that the words were put into my mouth, although it was I that spoke, and that everything was holy,—I perceived that it was the Son of God Himself who descended with such a resounding noise which by itself prostrated me to the ground, and that it was He who effected the prayer and thus declared it to be Jesus Himself. [56] I prayed for forgiveness that I had so long doubted it, and that in my thought I had demanded a miracle, which I now perceived to be improper. Thereupon I began to pray, and I prayed only for grace; more than this I could not express, but afterwards I prayed in addition to receive the love which is the work of Jesus Christ and not my own. In the meantime tremors often passed over me.

[57] Later on, about day-break, I fell asleep again, and then had continually in my thought how Christ conjoins Himself with men; holy thoughts came, but of such a nature that they are unfathomable, for I cannot in the least express by the pen what then took place; for I only know that I was in such thoughts.

[58] I then saw my father, dressed in a different costume, almost reddish. He called me to himself and took hold of my arms, which were in short sleeves, but with lace ruffles for cuffs; he took both cuffs and tied them with my ribbons. My wearing cuffs signifies that I am not of the Clergy, but that I am and ought to remain in civil service. He then asked me what I thought about this question, viz., that a certain king had granted leave to about thirty persons who belonged to the spiritual order, to get married and thus to change their estate. I replied that I had thought and written something

about this subject but that it has no relation to it. [59] Immediately afterwards I found myself able to answer, according to my conscience, that no one ought to be permitted to change his estate, no matter what it may be, to which he has devoted himself. He said that he also was of the same opinion, but I added that if the king had resolved upon it then the matter was settled. He said that he would present his vote in writing; if there are fifty [votes] then the matter is fixed. I noticed as a remarkable circumstance that I did not call him "my father" but "my brother." I afterwards wondered how this was: it seemed to me that my father was dead, and that this one, who is my father, thus must be my brother.

[60] I must not forget that it also entered my thoughts that the Holy Spirit wished to show me to Jesus and introduce me to Him, as a work which He had thus prepared, and that I ought not to ascribe anything to myself, but that everything is His, although He of grace appropriates the same to us.

I then sang the hymn I had chosen: "Jesus is my friend, the best one," n. 245.

[61] This much I have now learned in regard to what is spiritual, that there is nothing for it but to humble oneself, and not to ask for anything but the grace of Christ, and this in all humility. I had added what is of my own in order to obtain love, but this is presumptuous, for when a person possesses the grace of God, he gives himself up to Christ's pleasure, and acts according to His pleasure. One is happiest when he is in the grace of God. I must most humbly pray for forgiveness before my conscience can be satisfied, for I was in temptation before this had been done. The Holy Spirit taught me this, but I in my stupid understanding had neglected humility which is the foundation of everything.

[April] 7-8.

[62] Throughout the whole night I seemed to be going deep down, by ladders and other spaces, but quite safely and securely, so that the depth did not

bring me into any danger, and there occurred to me in the dream the verse,

"*Lowliness or other things, be they coming or . . . . .*"

[63] Afterwards I seemed to be at dinner in company with a number of persons at the house of a clergyman. I paid about a louis-d'or for the meal, and thus more than I ought, but when I was on my way from the place I had with me two vessels of silver which I had taken from the table. This troubled me and I tried to return them, and it seemed to me I had a plan to do so. This, I believe, signifies that in the temptation I had paid of my own, (it was the grace of God), and thus more than I ought to have done, (the grace of God), but that at the same time I had learned much in what is spiritual by this means, which is signified by the silver vessels which I wanted to return to the clergyman, that is, for the honor of God to give them back to the universal Church in some manner, which it seemed to me will also be done. [64] Afterwards I was in quite a large company at the house of another clergyman, where I seemed to

have been before. When we arrived it seemed to me that we were so many as to overwhelm the clergyman, and I did not like that we were so many as to cause him trouble. This signifies that I have so many unruly thoughts, which ought not to be, and that I cannot govern them, and they were compared to roving Poles and hussars, but they seemed to depart.

[65] I was also in this temptation, viz., that thoughts invaded me which I could not control; and this, indeed, so severely as to keep away every other thought but the one that they should be given free reins for once to oppose the power of the Spirit, which leads in a different direction. The temptation was so severe that if the grace of God had not been yet stronger I must have fallen therein, or else become insane. At times I was unable to force my thoughts to the contemplation of Christ whom I had seen, though only a little while. The movement and power of the Spirit came to me [to such an extent that I felt] that I would rather become insane [than to fall]. This referred to the second clergyman. [66] I may

compare this to a pair of scales for weighing: in the one is our own will and evil nature, in the other the power of God. In temptation our Lord so disposes these that at times they come into an equilibrium, but as soon as the first of the scales begins to weigh down heavier. He helps it up again. Such I have found to be the case, if I may speak of it in a worldly manner, from which it follows that this is far from being our own power, which draws everything downwards and is opposed rather than cooperating with the power of the Spirit, and consequently it is the work of our Lord alone, which He thus disposes.

[67] I then perceived that things were reproduced in my thoughts which had entered into them long before, so that I thereby found the truth of the Word of God that there is not the least word or thought which is not known to God, and if we do not receive the grace of God, we are responsible for it.

[68] This thing I have learned, that the only thing in this state,—I know not of any other,—is in humility to thank God for His grace, and to

pray for it, and to consider our own unworthiness and God's infinite grace.

[69] It was wonderful that I was able to have at one and the same time two thoughts quite distinct from one another,—the one for myself, which occupied entirely the thoughts of others; and at the side of this the thoughts of the temptation, in such a manner that nothing was powerful enough to drive them away. They held me captive so that I did not know whither to flee, for I carried them with me.

[70] Afterwards, because various things occurred to me which I had thought and fixed in my mind long ago, it was as if it had been said to me that I found reasonings by which to excuse myself.—and this also was a great temptation,— or to attribute to myself the good that I had done, or, to speak more correctly, the good which had been done through me; but the Spirit of God removed this also, and caused me to find it otherwise.

[71] This last [temptation] was more severe than the former in this respect that it reached to

the innermost, but over against this I received a yet stronger evidence of the Spirit, for at times I broke into a perspiration; what then came up [in my mind] was no longer anything that could condemn me, for I had the strong confidence that it was forgiven me, but that I should excuse myself and set myself free. Every now and then I burst into tears, not of sorrow but of inmost joy that our Lord has been willing to show such great grace to so unworthy a sinner. For the sum and substance of all I found to be this that the one and only thing is to cast oneself in humility upon the grace of our Lord, to perceive one's own unworthiness, and to thank God in humility for His grace; for if there is any glorification therein, looking towards one's own honor,—whether it be glorification of the grace of God or anything else,—it is impure.

[72] While the thought occurred to me, as it often does, if it should happen that anyone took me for a holy man, and therefore made much of me: nay, as is done by some simple-minded folks, if they were not only to venerate me but even adore me as a supposed saint; I then perceived

that in the zeal in which I then was, I would be willing to inflict upon him every evil, even unto the extreme, rather than [to permit] anything of such a sin to cleave to him. And [I recognized] that I must entreat our Lord with earnest prayers, that I may not have any share in so damnable a sin, or that it should cleave to me. [73] For Christ, in whom dwelleth the fulness of the Godhead, is alone to be adored in prayer, for He takes the greatest sinner to His grace, and does not regard our unworthiness, wherefore we must not in the prayer address ourselves to any one but Him. He is almighty, and is the only Mediator. What He does for the sake of others who have become saints, is His concern and not ours, that we should . . . [The rest of the sentence is obliterated].

[74] I perceived that I was unworthy above others and the greatest of sinners, for our Lord has granted me to go more deeply with my thoughts in certain matters than many others have done; and I perceived that here lies the very fountain of the sin, viz., in the thoughts which are brought to the work; so that in this manner my

sins come from a deeper source than in the case of many other persons. Herein I perceived my unworthiness and my sins to be greater than those of others; for it is not enough to call oneself unworthy, for this may be done while yet the heart is far away from it, and it may be a pretense, but to perceive that one is such, this is of the grace of the Spirit.

[75] Now while I was in the spirit, I thought and strove by means of my thoughts to gain a knowledge of how to avoid all that is impure, but I noticed nevertheless that on all occasions something from the love of self intruded itself and was turned about in the thought; as, for instance, when any one did not show the proper regard for me according to my own imagination, I always thought, "If you only knew what grace I am enjoying you would act otherwise," which at once was something impure having its source in the love of self. After a while I perceived this and prayed God to forgive it; and I then desired that others might enjoy the same grace, and perhaps they possess it or will obtain it. Thus I observed

clearly that there was still with me that pernicious apple which has not yet been converted, which is the root of Adam and of hereditary sin. Yea, and an infinite number of other roots of sin are with me.

[76] I heard a person at the table asking his neighbor the question whether any one who had an abundance of money could be melancholic. I smiled in my mind and would have replied,—if it had been proper for me to do so in that company, or if the question had been addressed to me,—that a person who possesses everything in abundance, is not only subject to melancholy, but is [exposed] to a still higher kind, that of the mind and the soul, or of the spirit which operates therein, and I wondered that he had proposed such a question. [77] I can testify to this so much the more, as by the grace of God there has been bestowed upon me in abundance everything that I require in respect to temporal things; I am able to live richly on my income alone, and can carry out what I have in mind, and still have a surplus of the revenue, and thus I can testify that the sorrow or melancholy

which comes from the want of the necessaries of life, is of a lesser degree and merely of the body, and is not equal to the other kind. The power of the Spirit prevails in the latter, but I do not know whether it is so also in the first kind, for it seems that it may be severe on bodily grounds; still, I will not enter further into this matter.

[78] I saw a bookshop, and immediately the thought struck me that my work would have greater effect than the works of others, but I checked myself at once by the thought that one person serves another and that our Lord has many thousand ways of preparing every one, so that every book must be left to its own merits, as a medium near or remote, according to the state of the understanding of every one. Nevertheless, the pride at once was bound to assert itself; may God control it, for the power is in His hands.

[79] I experienced so much of the Lord's grace, that when I determined to keep my thoughts in purity, I perceived the enjoyment of an interior gladness, but still there was a pain in the body, for it was not able to bear the heavenly joy of the soul;

I therefore left myself most humbly to the grace of God, that He might do with me according to His pleasure. May God grant me humility, that I may see my frailty, impurity, and unworthiness.

[80] During all these experiences I remained in the company of all my former associates, and no one could [perceive] any change in me whatsoever. This was of the grace of God, but I knew what . . . , not daring to tell that I realized the high grace that had been granted to me, for I perceived that this could serve no other purpose than to make people think this or that about me, each one for or against me, or perform any use, if privately . . . from the glorification of God's grace which . . . for the love of self.

[81] The best comparison I could make of myself was with a peasant who had been elevated to the power of a prince or king, so that he possessed everything his heart could wish for, but still there was something in him making him desire to learn that he himself knows nothing. By this comparison, however, one finds that ... it is Thy gracious hand which causes the entire joy, but still

I was anxious because he [I] cannot be content in this grace.

[April] 8-9.

[82] I seemed to have a dog on my knees, and I was astonished that it could speak. I asked about his former master, Swab. It was of a blackish color; it kissed me. I awoke, and prayed for the mercy of Christ, because I cherish much pride which flatters me.

Afterwards it seemed to me that on my day of prayers, which was yesterday, many things were packed up for the army.

[83] Afterwards there came in a young woman dressed in black, and said that I ought to travel to . . . then she came behind me, holding my whole back with her hand so firmly that I could not make a movement; I asked for help from a person near by, and he helped to get her away, but I was not able to move the arm myself. This referred to the temptation during the day, and means that I am not capable of doing anything good of myself. I

then heard as if someone were whistling, but he went away, and I was seized with a tremor.

[84] Afterwards I saw someone in St. Peter's church going into the vault underneath, where Peter lies. He was carried out, but it was said that yet another is hiding there.

It seemed that I was free to go in and out. May God lead me!

[85] Afterwards I saw all that was impure, and I acknowledged that I was impure from head to foot; I cried for the mercy of Jesus Christ.

Then it seemed that the words "I poor sinful creature" occurred to me; I also read the same the following day.

[April] 9-10.

[86] The whole day of the ninth I spent in prayer, songs of praise, reading the Word of God, and fasting, except in the morning when I was somewhat occupied with other things, until the same temptation arose, viz., that I was as it were forced to think what I did not wish to think.

[87] During the present night I slept very tranquilly. At three or four in the morning I woke up and lay awake, but as it were in a vision. I could look up and be awake when I wished to, so that I was not otherwise than awake, but as to the spirit there was an inward joy that could be felt all over the body. Everything seemed in a transcendent manner to [*abouterade?*]; it rose up, as it were, and concealed itself in something infinite as a centre, where love itself was, and it seemed as if it extended itself thence round about and thus down again. In this manner it moved by means of an incomprehensible circle from a centre which was love, round about and then back again. [88] In the mortal body this love which then filled me, was similar to the joy which a chaste man experiences when he is in genuine love and in the act itself with his spouse. Such an extreme delight was suffused over my whole body and this for a long while; this I have also experienced before, especially just before falling asleep and after the sleep for half an hour or even a whole hour. Now while I was in the spirit and yet awake,—for I

could open my eyes and be awake, and come back into that state again.—I saw and observed that the internal and real joy comes from this [love], and that in so far as one can be in it, in so far there is happiness, but that as soon as one comes into any other love, which does not concentrate in the former, one is out of the way of [true happiness]. [89] Thus when there was anything of the love of self, or any love which does not centre itself in this [love itself], then one was out of this [happiness]; a chill crept over me, and I as it were shivered a little, and I also felt a pain, from which I found that this was the source of my pains, sometimes, and also whence comes that great pain when the spirit is troubled: and that this finally remains as an eternal torment, and constitutes hell, when one unworthily receives Christ in the communion, for it is the Spirit which then torments one who is unworthy. [90] In the state I was in, I came still further into the spirit, and although I was awake I could not control myself, but there came as it were an overwhelming impulse to throw myself on my face and to fold my hands and to pray, as before, about my unworthiness, and to ask for grace with the deepest humility and reverence, that I as the greatest of sinners may receive forgiveness of sins. I then noticed that I was in the same state as during the night before last, but more I could not see, because I had become awake.

[91] I wondered at this, and then it was shown to me spiritually that a man in this state is like a person who has his head down and his feet up; and it occurred to me why Moses had to remove his shoes when he was to go into the presence of the Holy One; and also why Christ washed the feet of the apostles, and answered Peter that all is sufficient when the feet are washed. Then in the spirit I perceived that that which proceeds from the centre itself, which is love, is the Holy Spirit which is represented by the water, for there was mentioned water or a wave. [92] In short, when a person is in such a state as not to possess a love that centres upon self, but upon the common good—such as on the earth or in the moral world represents love in the spiritual world, and this not

for the sake of self or of society, but for the sake of Christ, who is love itself and the centre,—then he is in the right state. Christ is the ultimate end; all other things are mediate ends leading directly to Him.

[93] Afterwards I fell asleep, and I beheld one of my acquaintances sitting at a table. He greeted me, but I did not notice it at once, and before I had returned his greeting he became offended and gave me some harsh words. I wanted to excuse myself, and finally managed to say that I am often in deep thought and do not observe when someone greets me, and sometimes pass my friends on the street without seeing them. I appealed to an acquaintance, who was present, to bear witness, and he said that it was so, and I said that no one was more anxious to be polite and humble than I am, (God grant that this may be the case). This was on account of the night before, that I had been in other thoughts than I ought to have been, and may our Lord in His infinite grace excuse me. My friend, however, said nothing in reply, but still seemed satisfied, as I believed.

[April] 10-11.

[94] I came into a chamber below, where there were many persons, but I saw only a woman, dressed in black, not malicious; she walked far into a chamber, but I did not wish to go with her, though with her hand she beckoned me towards the door. Afterwards I went out and found myself several times stopped by a spectre which covered me over the whole of the back; finally it vanished.

[95] I came out, and then there came an ugly spectre who did the same; it was an ugly old man; at last I escaped from them. These were my thoughts on the previous day, when indeed I regarded myself as altogether too unworthy, and that I would not be able to endure throughout my life, but still trusted that God is mighty in everything and that His power will accomplish it; nevertheless there was something with me which prevented me from submitting to the grace of God as I ought, for Him to do with me according to His pleasure.

[96] When I came out I saw many persons sitting in a gallery, and, lo, a mighty stream of

water came pouring down through the roof, and it was so strong that it broke though everything in its way. There were some who tried to close the opening so that the water should not come in; others who tried to get away so that it should not reach them; others again tried to dissipate it into drops, and one who tried to divert it so that it would pass outside the gallery. This meant, I believe, the power of the Holy Spirit which flowed into the body and the thoughts: in part I impeded; in part I went out of its way; and in part I turned it aside, for the people signifies my own thoughts and will.

[97] Afterwards I came out thence, and in my thoughts I began as it were to measure and divide into parts that which proceeds from the centre to the circumference. It seemed to be heaven, for afterwards there appeared there a heavenly shining light: I may indeed reflect on this somewhat, but I dare not yet regard it as certain, for it refers to something which is to take place.

[98] While I was in the first infestation I cried to Jesus for help, and it went away; I also kept my

hands folded under my head, and then it did not return a second time. I was nevertheless in tremors when I awoke, and now and then I heard a dull sound, but I do not know whence it came.

[99] Afterwards, when I was awake. I began to think whether this might not be phantasy. I then noticed that the faith was faltering, but I prayed with folded hands that I might be strengthened in the faith, which also took place at once. I also fell into thoughts about my being more worthy than others, but I prayed in a similar manner and then it vanished at once. If therefore our Lord in the least withdraws His hand from a person, he is out of the right path and out of the faith itself, as has been the case with me who so manifestly has experienced it.

[100] This night I slept about eleven hours, and during the whole of the morning I was in my usual state of internal joy, and yet there was a certain pang along with it, which I supposed came from the power of the Spirit and from my own unworthiness. After a while by the assistance of God I came into thoughts such as these, that a

person ought to be content in all that the Lord pleases to do, because it is of the Lord, and that he should not then resist the Spirit when he receives from God the assurance that it is the grace of God which leads everything for our best. For since we are His, we must be content in what He pleases to do with that which is His own. Still we should pray for this to our Lord, for it is not in the least in our own powder.

[101] He then gave me His grace to this end. I reflected somewhat upon this and wanted to know why it is so, which was a sin. The thoughts should not go in that direction, but I must pray to our Lord for power to control them. It is enough that it is His pleasure. In everything we ought to call upon Him, pray to Him, give thanks to Him, and in humility acknowledge our unworthiness.

[102] I am still weak in body and thoughts, for there is nothing that I know except my own unworthiness, and that I am a miserable creature. This torments me, and I realize thence how unworthy I am of the grace that I have received.

[103] I observed also this that the stream of water which rushed down, had pierced the garments of a person who had been sitting there, as he was stepping out of the way. Perhaps there had fallen upon me a drop, which is pressing so hard. What, then, would have happened if the whole stream had reached me? I therefore took this for my

Motto:

God's will be done; I am thine and not mine own.

May God give His grace for this, for it is not mine.

[104] I perceived that a person may be in anguish spiritually, even though he is assured by the Spirit that his sins are forgiven and has the hope and confidence that he is in the grace of God. This may . . . [The last two words are obliterated.]

[April] 11-12.

[105] The whole night I was in a dream; I recollect only the smallest part. It was as if I was being instructed during the whole night in many

things which I do not remember. I was asleep about eleven hours. As far as I remember it seemed to me: 1. That substantial or essentials were mentioned, and that these should be cultivated and sought for; 2. Mention was made also of the thymus gland and renal glands, which I interpret as meaning that as the thymus gland secretes the impure serum from the blood, and the renal glands remit into the blood that which has been purified, so also it takes place in us, as I believe, spiritually.

[106] 3. My sister Caisa appeared; she pretended she was sick, and she threw herself down and screamed; but when our mother came, she put on quite a different face and talk; the interpretation of this will be given later. [107] 4. There was a minister preaching to a large congregation, and at the end he spoke personally against a certain individual, but whether that one was mentioned by name or not I do not know; but someone arose and rebuked the preacher, saying that such a thing ought not to be done. I was afterwards with them in a private company, and

then, on inquiry, it was said that the punishment for libelling anyone is a fine of three marks Swedish. He [the preacher] did not seem to know that it was thus punishable; it was said that the fine begins with one mark, then two marks, etc., which signifies that it is wrong to preach personally against anyone, or to speak or write, for it is punishable and libellous, for it affects a person's reputation and honor. [108] 5. Afterwards my knees moved of themselves, which may signify that I have become somewhat humble, as is also the case, by the grace of God, for which I give thanks most humbly.

[109] Afterwards I found in myself, and perhaps also from the third point in the dream, that in every single thought,—nay, even in such as we believe to be pure,—there is concealed an endless mass of sin and impurity, as also in every desire that enters' from the body into the thoughts, which spring from very deep roots. Although the thought may appear pure, underneath there is nevertheless the fact that a person thinks thus from fear, or hypocrisy, and many other causes, so

that on reflection it is found that no one can make himself so free from sin that there is not mixed into every thought much that is unclean or impure. It is therefore safest to acknowledge every hour and moment that one deserves the punishment of hell; but that it is the grace and mercy of God, which are in Jesus Christ, that overlook it. [110] Indeed, I have also observed that our whole will, which we have inherited and which is ruled by the body and introduces thoughts, is opposed to the spirit. For this reason there is a continual strife, and we cannot by any means unite ourselves with the spirit, which by grace is with us. And hence it is that we are as it were dead to all that is good, but to the evil we are [prone] of ourselves. A person should therefore at all times account himself guilty of innumerable sins, for the Lord God knows everything, and we ourselves know very little about those of our sins which enter only into the thoughts; but we become convicted of them only when they are ultimated in deed.

[April] 12-13.

[111] I perceived the fact to be,—as, indeed, I had thought through the spirit during the day, and as was also represented to me as it were by a kind of luminous writing,—that it is the will that has the chief direction over the understanding. When we inhale the breath the thoughts fly in from the body, and when we exhale the thoughts are as it were expelled and rectified, so that the very thoughts possess their alternations of activity like the respiration of the lungs. For the inspiration belongs to the will, and the expiration to nature, so that the thoughts have their alternations in every turn of respiration, because when wicked thoughts entered it was only necessary to draw in the breath, whereupon they ceased. [112] Hence also, may be seen the reason why, when in deep thought, the lungs are kept in a state of equilibrium and at rest, more according to nature, and that the inspirations are then more rapid than the expirations, when at other times the reverse is the case. Also that a person in a state of extasis holds the breath, the thoughts

then being as it were absent. Likewise in sleep, when both the inspiration and expiration are governed by nature, when that is represented which flows in from above. The same may also be deduced from the brain, that in the inspiration all the inmost organs, together with the brain itself, are expanded, and that the thoughts then have their origin and flux.

[113] Afterwards I came to a place where there were wonderfully large and tall windmills going at a terrible speed. I then came into a darkness, so that I crept on the ground, being afraid that one of the wings would catch me, which would have been the end of me. I did come beneath a wing which then stopped, and brought myself well within it, so that the wing helped me. It meant that during the day I had been in conflict with my thoughts, which are signified by the wings of the mill, and that sometimes I did not know whither I was tending. Yet, by the grace of God, they were calmed and I was brought forth safe and sound; wherefore, glory and praise to God, who looks not upon my weakness.

[114] Afterwards it seemed to me I was in company with some persons who appeared as if desirous to make gold, but they saw that they would have to climb up, which they were not able to do, and that otherwise it would be impossible to make gold; this continued for some time, until after a while I was together with two persons who nevertheless attempted to climb up, although our Lord was not with them. I said that it could not be done, and then went up before them; I had a rope, and pulled, but noticed that there was something beneath which pulled strongly against me; finally I saw that it was a man, but I was stronger and pulled up; then I was glad and said that it was as I had said. [115] It means, I believe, that the gold signifies what is good and pleasing to God; in order to gain it one must climb up, which is not in our power, even though we are able to do it by our own strength, and that we then find that there is something pulling strongly against us, but after a while there is victory, by the grace of God.

[116] Afterwards I remained long in the same thought, which became more and more luminously

red; this light signifies that the grace of God is written within it; and everything pointed to this, that we must actually do that which is good, by the grace of God and in faith, which God may grant, and to perform it; this is to make gold, for then we receive from our Lord everything that is needed and useful. This was very powerfully represented, that what is good ought to be put into effect, and that the gold consisted in this.

[117] Afterwards, when I got up, I was in a great fear of our Lord, as it were in a cold, which caused me to shiver at the least hint or thought that I was afraid of. It was the grace of God showing me that I must seek salvation in fear and trembling. And as I have my motto: "Thy will be done; I am Thine and not my own;" and as I have given myself away from myself to our Lord, may He therefore do with me according to His good pleasure. In the body there seemed to be something of discontent, but in the spirit there was joy, for it is the grace of our Lord that effects this. May God strengthen me therein!

[118] I was continually in a state of combat with double thoughts which were fighting one another. I pray Thee, O Almighty God, to grant me the grace to be Thine, and not mine own! Forgive me if I have said that I am Thine and not mine own; this belongs not to me, but to God. I pray *for the grace of being permitted to be Thine, and that I may not be left to myself.*

[April] 13-14.

[119] It seemed that the grace of the spirit labored with me during the whole night. I saw Hedwig, my sister, with whom I did not wish to have anything to do. This signifies that I must not touch the Economy of the Animal Kingdom, but leave it alone. Afterwards, when time dragged, it seemed that she first said to her children. Go out and read; and afterwards that we might play at backgammon or cards, whereupon they sat down to while away the time, and also to spend time at the meal. I believe this signifies that there is nothing wrong in this when it is done in the right way.

[120] Unæ accubebam, non pulchræ tamen mihi placebat; in loco ubi tetigi aliis similis erat, a fronte autem sicut dentes. Archenholtz fœminæ in forma videtur esse. Quid significaret nescio, sive non aliquam tangere, sive in politicis tacere, sive aliud.

[121] The whole day I was in double thoughts, which tried to destroy what was spiritual as it were by contemptuous abuse, so that I found that the temptation was very strong. By the grace of the Spirit I was led to fix my thoughts on a tree, then on the cross of Christ, and on Christ crucified; as often as I did this, the other thoughts fell down flat, as of themselves. [122] I bore down with this same thought so strongly, that it seemed to me I would crush the tempter by means of the cross and drive him away; then after a while I was free. Afterwards I had to fix my thoughts upon it so intently, that whenever I let it slip out of my thoughts and internal vision, I fell into temptation thoughts. Praise be unto God, who has given me this weapon! May God of His grace keep me in this, that I may always have my crucified Saviour

before my eyes. For I dared not look upon my Jesus, whom I have seen, because I am an unworthy sinner, but then I ought to fall upon my face, and it is Jesus who lifts me up to look upon Him, and therefore I must look upon Jesus crucified.

[April] 14-15.

[123] It seemed as if I were racing down a stairway; I touched each step only a little, and came safely down all the way without danger. There came a voice from my dear father, "You are making such a racket, Emanuel!" It was said he was angry, but it would pass over. This means that I made use of the cross too boldly, yesterday, but by the grace of God I came through without danger.

[124] I climbed up on a shelf, and broke off the neck of a bottle, from which some thick fluid came forth and covered the floor and then flowed down. I believe [this signifies] that yesterday, by the grace of God and not by my own power, a mass of evil was eradicated from my thoughts. I added

that which had been written, which means that which I am still to do.

[125] I heard a bear growling but did not see him. I dared not remain in the upper story, for there was a carcass there which he might scent. I therefore descended to one of the chambers of Dr. Moræus and shut the windows. This signifies temptation, not only to avarice but perhaps also to something else, and that I am engrossed in my anatomical speculations.

[126] Dr. Moræus seemed to be courting a pretty girl; he obtained her consent, and had permission to take her wherever he wanted. I teased her, saying that she was quite walling to say Yes, etc. She was a pretty girl, and grew taller and more beautiful. It meant that I was to inform myself on the subject of Muscles and study these.

[127] I had a preternaturally good and long sleep for twelve hours. On awakening I had before my eyes Jesus crucified and His cross. The spirit came with its heavenly and as it were ecstatic life so intensely, and permitting me to enter into it higher and higher, so that, if I had gone still

higher, I would have been dissolved by this veritable life of joy.

[128] It then appeared to me in the spirit that I had gone too far; that in my thoughts I had embraced Christ on the cross when I kissed His feet, and that I then removed myself thence, and falling upon my knees and praying before Him crucified. It seemed that the sins of my weakness are forgiven as often as I do this. It occurred to me that I might have the same with a graven image before the eyes of my body, but I found that this would be far from right and, indeed, a great sin.

[April] 15-16.

[129] It seemed as if I was climbing up a ladder from a great deep; others, women whom I knew, came after me. I stood still and purposely frightened them, and then went up. I came up against a green earth-wall and lay down; the others came after me. I greeted the women and they sat down beside me: one was young and the other a little older. I kissed the hands of both and did not know which one of them I should love. It

was my thoughts and mental work [*ouvrage d'esprit*], of two kinds, which finally came up with me, and which I received again, and greeted, and took up again.

[130] Afterwards I came to a place where many male persons were assembled; a great crowd of handsome young folks in one place in a flock; fresh numbers joined them, among others Henning Gyllenborg on horseback. I went to meet him, kissed him, and stood by him. It signifies that I have returned to the things of my memory and imagination, and am again greeting them; consequently that I am returning to the superior and inferior faculties.

[131] Afterwards I returned home and was in my own house. I received many visitors. I knew that I had hidden away a pretty little woman and a boy and kept them hidden. There was moreover but a slight store of provisions, and I was not yet willing to bring out my silver plate before I should treat them; nor was I willing to lead the guests into an inner magnificent chamber which was well furnished within. This signifies that I have come

home to myself again, and that I have acquired the knowledge which I have now written down here, and that in time I may make use of it, and bring out the silver and lead them into the handsome chamber.

[132] It seemed that I was accusing some one, but I do not remember how; in the end, however, I crossed out and excused something, because he himself had said so, but the words were buried. It signifies that I had accused myself, but excused myself because I had admitted everything.

[133] [I heard] mentioned the words *Nicolaiter*, and *Nicolaus Nicolai*; I do not know if this signifies my new name. The most remarkable fact was this that I now represented the internal man and was as it were another than myself, so that I saluted my own thoughts, frightened them, the things of my own memory, that I accused another one. Thus now there has been a change so that I represent the internal man, who is opposed to another person, for I have prayed to God that I may not be mine own, but that God may please to let me be His.

This has lasted now for twenty-one days.

[134] I found later on that most of this had a different meaning: 1. The two women signified that I would rather remain in philosophical studies than to be in spiritual ones, as rather showed my inclination. 2. My kissing Henning Gyllenborg, and seeing so many people, meant that I not only delighted in being in worldly society but also wished to boast of my work. 3. Nicolaus Nicolai was a philosopher who every year sent loaves of bread to Augustus. First, therefore, this, that I found it my duty to reconcile myself again to our Lord, because in spiritual things I am a stinking carcass. [135] On this account I went to [our Swedish] Envoy, Preis, and he called upon Pastor Pambo in order that I might again receive the Lord's Supper, which was also granted. I met him at the house of the Envoy and went in with him, which was of the Providence of our Lord. I dined the same day with the Envoy, Preis, but had no appetite.

On the 17th I received the Lord's Supper from Pastor Pambo.

[April] 17-18.

[136] I had frightful dreams; dreamt that the executioner roasted the heads which he had struck off, and for a long time he put the roasted heads one after another into an empty oven, which nevertheless was never filled. It was said that this was his food. He was a big female; he laughed, had a little girl with him.

[137] Afterwards I dreamt that the Evil One carried me into various deep places and bound me; I do not remember it all. I was cast, bound, everywhere in hell.

[138] I dreamt that a great procession was arranged, from which I was excluded, and that I should have come away thence. But I labored to get there, and sat down, but they advised me to go away, and I went. Nevertheless, I had another place where I could see it, but it had not yet arrived.

[139] I am certain, however, that God grants grace and pity to all poor sinners who are willing to be converted and who are willing in steadfast faith to take refuge in His inconceivable mercy

and in the merit of the Saviour Jesus Christ. I therefore assure myself of His grace and leave myself in His protection, because I firmly believe that I have received forgiveness for my sins. This is my consolation, and may God confirm it for the sake of Jesus Christ.

[140] I was this day by turns in interior anxiety and sometimes in despair; nevertheless I was assured of the forgiveness of my sins. Thus at intervals a heavy perspiration broke out upon me until 10 o'clock, when with the help of God I fell asleep. Then it seemed to me it was said that something will be given from within. I slept for an hour and a half, although in the night I had slept for more than ten hours. By the grace of God I have had a preternatural sleep, and this for an entire half year.

[April] 18-19.

[141] It seemed to me that we were laboring for a long time to bring in a cabinet, in which were kept more precious things; indeed, a long time, as it was at Troy. Finally they went below it and

shaved it off; afterwards it was carried in as if in triumph, and they kept on sawing and sawing. It signifies how we must labor in order to gain heaven.

[142] It seemed I had a cheap watch with me, although at home I had precious watches which I was not willing to exchange for golden ones. It signifies that I may obtain knowledges, of a noble kind, upon which I may use my time.

[143] It seemed to me I was being wrapped about, below, in folds of blankets, which were wound around in various ways, and at the same time there came as it were ———. This signifies that I am being continually protected, so as to remain in the right purpose.

[144] There was a dog following me; he was very well mannered and of a dark brown color; he rose up when any animal approached; when near water he went into it in order to explore its depth. Perhaps this signifies the dog of Tobit.

[145] I saw in a window a singular animal; it was lively and also of dark brown color, and it came in through another window. It had

something on its back which was rubbed off and was changed into a handkerchief. I looked at it and still saw it a little, but could not show it to anyone else. There was an apothecary's shop inside. I asked if I should shoot the animal. This may signify that I am going to be instructed as to what may serve for reformation, etc.

[146] Afterwards it seemed as if it would be shown to me that I should be told or be given to understand when I would be in danger of going astray.

[147] I saw König and Prof. Winbom approaching, viz., that I was going to live with them, on a week-day with those who are not Christians, for König was said not to be a Christian, Winbom approaching signifies Sundays.

[148] This day also I have been somewhat disturbed in my mind, because against my will the thoughts were flying for and against, and I could not control them. I was at Divine worship, and found that the thoughts in matters of faith, respecting Christ, His merit, and the like, even though they be favorable and confirmatory,

nevertheless cause a disturbance, and permit contrary thoughts to enter in, such as cannot be kept out, when a man desires to believe from his own understanding and not from the grace of the Lord. [149] At last it was granted me by the grace of the spirit to receive faith, without reasoning, an assurance of it. I then saw my own confirmatory thoughts as it were beneath me; I laughed at them in my mind, and still more at those thoughts which offended and opposed them. Then only did I receive peace. May God strengthen me herein, for it is His work, and mine so much the less as my own thoughts, nay, even the best of them destroy more than they promote it. A person must laugh at himself as well when he thinks in opposition as also when he desires to confirm with his understanding that which he believes. It is therefore something higher,—I know not whether it be the highest,—when a man receives the grace no longer to mix up his own understanding in matters of faith. [150] It seems, however, that our Lord in the case of certain persons permits assurances to precede that which concerns the understanding. Blessed are those who believe and do not see; concerning this I have written clearly in the Prologue, nos. 21, 22; yet of my own self I could not have remembered this or discovered it, but it was the grace of God that wrought it without my being conscious thereof, as I afterwards found from the very effect and the change in my whole interior being. It is therefore the grace and the work of God, to whom be everlasting glory. [151] From this I can perceive how difficult it is for the learned,—more, indeed, than for the unlearned,—to come to such a faith, and thus overcome themselves so as to be able to laugh at themselves, for the adoration of one's own understanding must first of all be abolished and thrown down; and this is the work of God and not of man. It is, moreover, the work of God to keep a person in such a state. This faith, therefore, becomes separated from our understanding, and resides above it.

[152] This is pure faith; the other is impure, so long as it mixes itself with our own understanding; we must make our understanding

captive to the obedience of faith. We should believe because it has been said by Him who is God over all, the Truth itself. This, perhaps, is what is meant by the teaching that we should be like children. Much of that which I have seen agrees with this, and perhaps also this that so many heads were roasted and thrown into the oven, and that it was the food of the Evil One.

[153] That confirmations becloud the faith, may be seen from this that the understanding never reaches further than probabilities, in which there is ever as it were a trying of major or minor lemmas. And therefore the confirmations from self intelligence are always subject to doubt, which darkens the light of faith. This faith, therefore, is purely the gift of God, which a man receives if he lives according to the commandments of God and diligently prays to God for it.

[April] 19-20.

[154] I experienced a totally different kind of sleep; I dreamt a great deal, after which tremors

came upon me, but I could not recollect anything, for each time I tried, it escaped me.

[155] I held my hands clasped, and on awakening it seemed to me that they were pressed together by a hand or finger; which by the help of God signifies that our Lord has heard my prayers.

[156] Afterwards in a vision, which was neither a state of sleep, nor of wakefulness, nor of ecstasy, it occurred to me that King Charles [XII] the first time had fought in vain, and that afterwards in his second battle with the Saxons he was victorious, and was covered with blood. And afterwards I dreamt that the Muses also were victorious; which signifies that by the grace of God I have gained the battle, and that the blood and merit of Jesus have helped me; and that in my studies I shall gain my object..

[157] I now arose, a whole God up. God be thanked and praised! *I do not wish to be mine own; I am certain and believe that Thou, O God, wilt let me be Thine in all the days of my life and wilt not take away from me Thy Holy Spirit which strengthens and upholds me.*

[158] This day I have been in most severe temptation, so that when I thought of Jesus Christ there came at once ungodly thoughts, which I could not be blamed for, as it seemed to me, I beat myself, but I can confess that I was never of better courage than this day, and was not in the least downhearted or pained as on previous days, although the temptation was most severe. The reason is that our Lord has given me the firm faith and confidence that; He will help me for the sake of Jesus Christ and on account of His promise, so that I then experienced the efficacy of such a faith.

[159] My mood was indeed such that I was so incensed against Satan, that I wanted to beat him with the weapons of faith; from this may be perceived the efficacy of the right kind of faith without reasoning or confirming by means of one's own reasons; but it is the grace of God alone. If this temptation had taken place previously, I would have become altogether downhearted. Yet I was afraid that I had offended our Lord by forcing [Him] as it were to set me free, on account of which I asked His forgiveness with all the

humility of which I was capable. This probably signifies Charles XII, who was covered with blood.

[April] 21-22.

[160] It seemed to me as if I had gone astray in the dark, and had not gone out in company with others. I groped for the walls, and after a while I came to a beautiful house, where there were some people who wondered at my coming that way. They met me and said that this was not the way. I said that in the wind [?] perhaps there was an opening this way, which they denied. It signifies that this day I had gone astray the worst.

[161] Then there was a big dog that came in beneath the cover of the bed where I was lying, and he licked my neck. I was afraid he would bite me, but it did not happen, and it was said he would not bite me. It signifies the thoughts aside, which I have entertained, [on account of which] I was precluded from thinking of what was holy.

[162] Afterwards I was together with some comedians. Some! one said that a Swede had arrived and wished to see me. We drove in, and a

large staircase was made ready for him. It was a dog wrapt up, with a pup suckling. It signifies my terrible thoughts. Something similar was hanging from a fishing rod and could not be removed; finally in another room it was torn off. It signifies what I will be liberated from.

[163] In a vision it seemed to me as if something was torn to pieces in the air. It may signify that my double thoughts will be torn asunder.

As I was awakening there were heard the words "all grace" which signifies that everything that has taken place is grace and for my best.

[164] Afterwards I came into a state of hesitation,— because I seemed to be so far separated from God, that I could not yet think of Him in a living manner,—whether I should not turn my journey homewards. There came a mass of involved reasonings and motions of the body, but I gathered courage and experience and perceived that I had come here in order to do the very best and to promote the glory of God, that I had received talent, that everything had helped to

this purpose; that the spirit had been with me from my youth unto this end. I considered myself unworthy to live if I had gone otherwise than the right way, and thus I laughed at the other seductive thoughts. [165] Thus as to pleasure, wealth, high position, which I had pursued, I perceived that all was vanity, and that he is the more happy who is not in possession thereof, but is contented, than the one who does possess them. And therefore I laughed at all confirmatory reasonings, and thus by the help of God I came to a resolution. May God help!

I seemed to hear a hen cackling, as takes place at once after she has laid an egg.

[166] I noticed, further, that faith does indeed consist in an assured confidence which is received from God, but nevertheless it consists in the work, that a man is to do what is good to his neighbor, each one according to his talent, and this more and more; and that it is to be done from the faith that God has thus commanded, without further reasoning-, but to do the works of charity under the obedience of faith, even though it may be

against the kist of the body and its persuasions. And therefore a faith without works is not the right kind of faith: one must actually forsake himself.

[April] 22-23.

[167] Bad dreams, about dogs that were said to be my own countrymen, and which licked my neck but did not bite; with other things, as to how I wanted to do something with two persons, but nothing took place. In the morning I fell into terrible thoughts, as also during the day, that the Evil One had taken possession of me, yet with the consolation that he was outside and soon would let me go. [168] Just as I was in damnable thoughts, the worst kind that could be, in that very moment Jesus Christ was presented vividly before my internal eyes, and the operation of the Holy Spirit came upon me, so that hence I could know that the devil was gone. The next day I was now and then in a state of infestation and in double thoughts and in strife. After dinner I was mostly in a

pleasant humor, though engaged in worldly things. Then I travelled to Leyden.

[April] 23-24. In Leyden.

[169] It seemed to me that I was fighting with a woman while I was fleeing; she drove me into a lake and up again; finally I struck her as hard as I could with a plate in the forehead and squeezed her face, so that she seemed to be conquered. This signified my infestations and my struggle with my thoughts, which I had vanquished.

[170] It seemed as if someone said the words *interiorescit* [he is becoming more internal] and *integratur* [he is being made whole]; which signifies that by my infestations I am becoming more purified.

[171] Afterwards something was being dictated to me during the whole night, something holy which ended with the words "sacrarium et sanctuarium." Videbar in lecto cum foemina, et dixi, si non "sanctuarium" dixisses, fecissemus. Ab illa me averti, illa manu sua meum tetigit, quod crevit in tantum quantum usque ante. Me

converti, idque admovi; se flectebat, tamen intrudit. Dixit illud nimis longum esse. Interea reflexi hujus facti eventum foetus esse debiturum, et abivi "en merveille."

Ad lectum erat speculatrix, quoedam, sed prima abivit.

[172] Significat amorem sancti maxime ultimum, omnis enim amor inde originem suam trahit; est series: in corpore est actualiter in projectione seminis, cum totum adest et purum, significat amorem sapientiæ. Hoc pro veritate, sed quia quoedam subauscultabat, et non prius factum est quam illa abiverit, significat quod de illa re tacendum sit, quodque neminis ad aures veniret; nam intellectu mundano impurum tametsi in se purum est.

[173] Afterwards I slept a little, and it appeared to me as if there was flowing a quantity of oil with a little mustard mixed with it. This may signify my life that is coming, and it may mean pleasantness mixed with adversity, or it may mean a medicine for me.

This took place at Leyden, in the morning of April 24.

[April] 24-25. In Amsterdam.

[174] During the whole night, for about eleven hours, I was in a strange trance, neither asleep nor awake. I knew all that I dreamt, but my thoughts were kept bound, which at times caused me to sweat. I cannot describe the nature of that sleep, during which my double thoughts were as it were separated from each other or torn asunder. [175] Among other things I dreamt that I spoke several times with King Charles XII, and that in speaking with me he said everything in broken French, at which I wondered, but did not understand. Even when I was speaking with others and supposed that he did not hear me, he was present beside me, so that I was ashamed that I had spoken. This signifies that God is speaking with me, and that I comprehend only the least portion thereof, because it consists in representations, of which as yet I understood very little. And that He hears and observes everything

that is said and every thought that any one has. Indeed, there is not a thought that can escape but that He sees it; in fact, everything, ten thousand times more than I can perceive [in] myself.

[176] It seemed as if a number of women and men were sitting in a ship, ready to depart. One of them was holding my dog, which I took away from him. He showed me the way home into a beautiful chamber, where there was wine. This perhaps signifies that I should send my work over to England, and that on the same day I should amuse myself, as also took place, at [the house] of Mr. Hinr. Posch.

[April] 25-26. At The Hague.

[177] [I enjoyed] a delightful and precious sleep for about eleven hours, with several representations; it was as if a married woman was pursuing me, but I escaped. It signifies that the Lord is saving me from temptations and persecutions.

[178] A married woman wanted to have me, but I liked an unmarried one; the former one became

angry and persecuted me, but I nevertheless gained the unmarried one and was with her and loved her. It may signify my thoughts.

[179] It was a woman who owned a very beautiful estate in which we walked about, and I was to marry her. She signified piety, and also, I believe, wisdom, which owned these possessions, Etiam cum illa eram illamque more solito amabam, quod vicem ipsius conjugii obtinere videbatur.

[180] It was also represented to me in a certain way that I ought not to contaminate myself by [reading] other books, treating of theology and such subjects; because this I have in the Word of God and from the Holy Spirit.

[April] 28-29.

[181] Last night it seemed to me that I saw King Charles XII, to whom I had once dedicated my work, but it now seemed to me that he had risen from the dead, and that I went out, and now wished to dedicate to him as if he were like another [living] person.

[182] I was walking along a road and came to a cross-road, on which I was directed to proceed. I also went up, but it seemed to me there were only a few days left, so I went back in the place; there was a mass of people. I wanted to go out but was very much crowded.

[183] I gave some fruits to a gardener to sell. He sold them and returned two carolines to me, but it was said that he had kept thirteen dalers for himself, but I did not care about it.

[184] Videbar mihi aquam mingere, foemina in lecto spectante; obesa erat et rubeda. Postea mammam illius tangebam, nec illa se retraxit; secreta sua et turpe quoddam mihi ostendit; illæ nihil facere volebam,

[185] All this, as it seems to me, signifies that I ought to employ my remaining time upon what is higher, and not write about worldly things, which are far beneath, but [write] about that which concerns the very centre of everything, and that which concerns Christ. May God be so gracious as to enlighten me further in regard to my duty, for I

am still in some darkness as to whither I ought to turn.

[186] It seemed that some one had written briefly to King Frederic; it seemed brief to him, and he commanded some persons to travel to the one [who had written], who at first seemed to be a woman but afterwards appeared like a small man, to worry that' one in various ways with love-intrigues and the like. They did their best, but I saw that they had not hurt him or done him any injury. He said that now, between the thirty sixth and thirty-seventh day, (which was the day since my temptation), he wished to borrow a heap and go to heaven, without paying those from whom he had borrowed. This I told to the Swab, that he should report it to the King. All this seemed to signify that if I go on with the other [work] which I have proposed to myself, I have borrowed a heap from what is spiritual, in order thereby to go to heaven, which I was not willing to pay, unless very tardily.

[April] 30-May 1.

[187] I saw someone on guard with a sword; it was pointed and sharp, and there was something sticking to the sleeve of his coat. I was in danger from him, for I saw that he was somewhat drunk and consequently might do harm. It signifies that on the previous day I had drunk a little more than I ought, which is not of the spirit, but of the flesh, and therefore sinful.

[188] Afterwards it seemed to me that I had with me Eliezer, my deceased brother, who was being attacked by a wild boar that held him fast and bit him. I tried to drag the animal down with a hook, but could not. Afterwards I went up, and saw that he was lying between two boars which were eating his head. I could not get anyone to help him; I ran past. This, as I believe, signifies that on the previous day I had indulged my appetite and had partaken too freely of the necessaries of life, which is also a work of the flesh and not of the spirit; for such is the life of swine, and is forbidden by Paul; it is called feastings.

[189] On the following day I was more on my guard, but I came into a rather strong temptation. That now and henceforth I must thus forcibly govern my appetite, this brought me into a strange condition, and as it were into a state of chagrin; but I was quickly delivered from it after I had prayed and sung a hymn; especially as I do not wish to be mine own, but to live as a new man in Christ.

[190] Afterwards for several days in succession I was generally for some hours in a state of spiritual anxiety, without being able to tell the cause, although I seemed to be assured of the grace of God. After dinner, however, I was in quite a great state of happiness and spiritual peace,

[191] When I started on my journey from The Hague in the ship from Maasland, which took place on the thirteenth of May, it seemed that my brother Jesper had been put in prison on my account, and also another person. I had put something into a carriage and imported it, for which I seemed to be responsible. There came judges who were to sentence him, holding in their

hands two written papers. In the meanwhile I beheld some birds which came flying towards me, but I hit them on the neck with a sharp knife so that they died. Then the judges came and released my brother Jesper, whom I thereupon kissed and rejoiced over. It signifies that I had been running wild in my thoughts, but that with the help of the Spirit I had killed them, and that 1 therefore was declared free.

[192] While in Harwich, on my arrival in England, I slept only a few hours, and then there appeared many things which may concern my work here. This took place on May 4-5, according to the English calendar. [193] 1) It seemed that I had lost a banknote, and the person who found it got only nine stivers for it. The same was the case with another person who had also found such a banknote, which was bought for nine stivers only. I observed, jokingly, that this was *"pietasteri."* It probably showed what is the state in England, partly honest, partly dishonest. [194] 2) There were some who admired my copperplate engravings, which were well executed, and they

desired to see my first sketches, as if I could sketch them as they were executed. It may signify that my work will gain approbation, although they believe that I was not able to do it. [195] 3) I received a small letter, for which I paid nine stivers; when I opened it I found within a large book with blank paper. In the middle there were many beautiful drawings, but the rest was blank paper. A woman was sitting at my left hand; she moved over to my right side and began to turn over the leaves of the book, and the drawings appeared. It seemed to me that the meaning of the letter was that while in England I should order a lot of such drawings or patterns to be made. The woman had a rather broad neckcloth, and was altogether bare on both sides all the way down; the skin was shining as if glazed, and on the thumb there was a miniature painting. It may signify that with the help of God I may while in England execute a lot of handsome designs in my work; and that afterwards speculation will turn to *priora*, while before it has been in *posteriora*, as seems to be signified by her change of position.

[196] 4) It seemed as if I had received orders to accompany Bergenstierna on a commission, and that money had been granted for the purpose. The commission, with which I was quite pleased, seemed to be on the other side of Sicily, but I thought that I would have to be on guard against scorpions there. It may signify something which may be committed to me after my work has been finished; that perhaps I am going to effect it in some other place, and perhaps in some other cause.

[197] May 5-6, in London. I got a whipping from a large man, and I took it for my good. Then I was about to get up on a horse to ride alongside a carriage, but the horse turned his head and got hold of me by my head and held me. What this signifies I do not know. I may have done something wrong to a pious shoemaker who was with me on the journey, and with whom I was then lodging; or [it may mean] that I had not been thinking of my work.

[198] *Summa summarum*: (1) There is nothing else but grace, by means of which we may be

saved. 2) The grace is in Jesus Christ who is the throne of grace. 3) It is the love of God in Christ by which salvation is effected. 4) And that a man then allows himself to be led by the spirit of Jesus. 5) Everything that comes from ourselves is dead, and is nothing but sin and worthy of eternal damnation. 6) For nothing good can come except from the Lord.

[May] 19-20. In London.

[199] On the twentieth I had intended to go to the Lord's Supper in the Swedish Church, because recently I had fallen into many pernicious thoughts, so that I observed that the body is continually rebellious, which was moreover represented to me by scum which must be removed. On Sunday in the morning there came quite clearly from the Spirit into my mouth, that this [the Holy Supper] is the manna which comes from heaven. I was neither in a state of sleep nor of wakefulness, but it came quite clearly into my thought and mouth that it signifies Christ in the Lord's Supper. On the previous day I had been so

prepared that I enjoyed an interior tranquillity and peaceful contentment in the Lord's disposition; and the whole time I felt the powerful influence of the Holy Spirit, a joy and an earthly kingdom of heaven, which filled the whole body.

[200] Nevertheless I could not keep control of myself so as not to desire the sex, although not with the intention of proceeding to effect; yet in the dream it did not seem to be altogether contrary to the dispensation of God. I was in the company of Prof, Oelreich in various places. I had never been warned against this, as I had been warned against other things that I had committed. Nevertheless it happened,—as had been represented to me some days before in a dream,—that in one and the same day I was twice in danger of my life, as also happened, so that if God had not then been my protection, I would have lost my life in two places. The particulars I will not describe.

[201] The internal joy remained so intense, however,—especially when I was by myself, alone, without company, in the mornings, and evenings,

and days,—that it may be compared to a heavenly joy here on the earth. This I hope to retain as long as by the grace of our Lord alone I walk in the pure path and have the right intention, for it vanishes if I turn aside to seek my pleasure in worldly things. God knows best whether the interior principle, which is the influx of the Spirit of God, is constantly with me. Every least degree of exaltation is that of which it is sensible, and therefore I thought that since I enjoy this heavenly joy, why should I seek for worldly pleasure which by comparison is nothing, is inconstant, hurtful, opposing, and destructive of the heavenly joy.

[202] By various providential dispensations I was led to the chapel belonging to the Moravian Brethren, who claim to be the real Lutherans and that they are conscious of the operation of the Holy Spirit, as they tell one another; and that they look only to the grace of God, and the blood and merit of Christ, and that they work in innocent simplicity. Concerning this I shall speak more fully another time, but it may not yet be permitted

for me to join brotherhood with them. Their chapel was represented to me three months ago, just as I afterwards saw it, and all there were dressed like clergymen.

[June] 11-12.

[203] I was thinking about those who resist the Holy Spirit, and about those who suffer themselves to be governed by it. There appeared to me a man in white having a sword; another person approached to attack him and was wounded by his sword; he renewed the attack but was wounded quite severely about the ear and the temples. Still another came to fight against him, but he also was run through so that the blood appeared. I had a long spear and was thinking that if he should come against me, I would hold the spear in front of me, but just as he was not far from me I saw that he threw down the sword and went away. As I was wondering at this, I noticed that some one was walking before me, and that he had reversed his sword to give it to him and surrender

unconditionally, which was the reason for his reversing his sword.

June 15-16. The sixteenth was a Sunday.

[204] My past life was represented to me, and how afterwards I walked where there were precipices on all sides, and that I turned back. Then I came to a very lovely grove, planted everywhere with most beautiful fig trees in fine growth and order. On one of them there seemed to remain dried-up figs. The grove was surrounded with moats, except on the side where I was. I wanted to pass over a foot bridge, which was high, and with earth and grass on the top, but I dared not on account of the danger. [205] At some distance from it I saw a large and quite beautiful palace with wings, where, it seemed to me, I desired to take lodgings in order to have the prospect of the grove and the moats always in view. A window was open far down in one of the wings, and I thought I should like to have my room there. It signifies that on the Sunday I should be in what is spiritual, which is meant by

the lovely grove; the palace may mean the plan of my work, which looks toward the grove, whither I intend to look by means of it.

[June] 20-21.

[206] It seemed that a deliberation was going on as to whether I should be admitted to the society there, or to one of their councils. My father came out and said to me that what I had written about Providence was the finest. I called to mind that it was only a small treatise. Afterwards, one night, I was found in the Church, but I was naked, having nothing on but the shirt, so

[June] 26-27.

that I did not dare to come forward. This may mean that I am not yet clothed and prepared as I need to be.

[207] I was in a place together with many persons. I went past my garden which looked quite badly,—no doubt in comparison with the heavenly [garden]. Then for a long time I heard the roar of cannons being fired against the enemy, in various

directions, and it seemed to me that the enemy was being beaten. There also came a message that the Danes were attacking with ten thousand men; the battle was mostly with sword-hilt [in hand]; they were altogether beaten. There was also [a battle] in another place, and I wanted to drive out to view the battle fields. Where I was there were a number of persons who wanted to run away, because they were of the Danish party, but I advised them to remain, as they were in no danger, but only a Danish soldier was. [208] I saw afterwards that I was protected by a large screen;—that there was something the matter with my left foot, of which I had not been conscious; but it was bound up and would soon be right again.—In a large cage there was a little bird, which had been concealed for a long time, but still it lived and had food and drink, and went in and out of the cage.—I saw Eric Benzelius wearing a wig with two curls behind; he walked about tired and old. I went with him and saw that he walked into a church and sat down in the very lowest place.

July 1-2.

[209] Something quite wonderful happened to me. I came into violent tremors, one after another, about ten or fifteen in succession, like those [which came upon me] on the occasion when Christ did to me the Divine honor [of manifesting Himself]. I expected to be thrown on my face, as on the former occasion [see nos. 51-56], but this did not take place. At the last of the tremors I was raised up, and with my hands I felt the back [of somebody]; I passed my hands over the whole of the back and in front on the breast. He at once lay down, and in front I saw also a face, but quite obscurely. I was then standing on my knees, and I was thinking whether I should lie down beside him, but this did not take place, as if it was not permitted. The tremors came, all of them, from the body below, up to the head. [210] This took place in a vision, when I was neither awake nor asleep, for I had all my thoughts collected. It was the interior man, separated from the exterior, that sensated it. When I was altogether awake similar tremors came over me several times. It must have

been an holy angel [and not Christ Himself], since I was not thrown on my face. What it may signify is known best to our Lord. It seemed as if it had been told me before that I should have some [reward] for my obedience or for some other reason. The grace of God is being shown both to the interior and to the exterior man with me. To God alone be praise and honor!

[211] From what followed and from other things I perceive that this signified that I am going to discover truths concerning the internal sensations, but as it were on the back, and obscurely as to their front; because before this happened it seemed as if I were told that it was an announcement in regard to that in which I have hitherto worked; afterwards also it appeared to me that I went to exchange my poor stivers for better coin, and then a little gold was given to me, although there was some copper at the side of it.

July 3-4.

[212] It was with a special tenderness that I as it were said farewell to her [*i. e. the former work*],

kissing her, when another appeared at a little distance. The effect was that while in a wakeful state I was in a continual burning of love. Nevertheless it was said, and regrets were expressed, that it was not better understood. This signifies that I have now finished writing on the senses in general, and on the operation of the interior faculties, which cannot be comprehended in the form that has been sketched out; and that I now approach the second part, which is the brain.

July 7-8.

[213] I saw how everything in an oblong globe concentrated itself upwards in the highest part of the globe, while in the lowest part there was as it were a tongue, which afterwards was spread out. It signifies, as I believe, that the inmost was a sanctuary and as a centre of the globe beneath, and that such things as are indicated by the tongue must as to a great part be considered. I believe that I am destined for this, as was infallibly the signification of the "sanctuary" that I had to do with. This is confirmed by the fact that

all the objects of the sciences are represented to me by means of women; as also that there was a deliberation as to whether I should be admitted into the Society where my father was.

[214] There came to me also the assuring thoughts that the Son of God was the love which, in order to do good to the human race, took upon Himself their sins, even to the most severe punishment; for if the justice existed, the mercy must be effected by means of the love.

[July] 9-10.

[215] I was in company with the King and conversed with him, who was afterwards in a chamber. Later on I was with the princes, his sons, with whom I became acquainted. They were speaking among themselves about me. I said that I felt bashful from love and veneration. As I started to leave I noticed that the table had been set by the queen. I was not dressed as was due, because as before I had hastily taken off my white jacket, and I wanted to go up and put it on again. I spoke with my father who kissed me because I

reminded him not to swear. Meanwhile the Queen came up with her suite. This signifies that I am becoming acquainted with God's children, for during the day I chose other lodgings for myself.

[July] 14-15.

[216] I was conversing with Brita Behm who, as it seemed to me, had given birth to a son; yet, as Schwede had been dead for a long time, I wondered how this could be. The child died, however, and in its place were the two Rosenadlers. She took me into a large and costly carriage, of surpassing magnificence, and conducted me to Count Horn. [217] A meal was being prepared there; I went away but intended to return. I was flying evenly, but came to a fine looking town which I saw; I noticed that I was flying in the wrong direction, and I turned back. This signifies my work on the interior senses and the brain, which was compared to Brita Behm's child. That I drove in a costly carriage to Count Horn, who was President of the Court of Chancery and Prime-minister of the realm, and then [flew]

to another town, means perhaps that I had proceeded too close to the soul.

[218] I crossed a sheet of water on a foot bridge; there was a ship near by; I came to a hole. I then thought of bread, that large and small loaves were brought there every day. It may signify the Lutheran Church. Christ is compared to the spiritual bread.

[July] 21-22.

[219] I saw a congregation where every one had a small crown on his head, and two persons were standing in front, having quite large and magnificent crowns. One of them spoke in joy, and it was half in French, half in German. *It signified those who had received the crowns of martyrs*, concerning whom I had been thinking during the day. But I do not know who the two [in front] were, or whether one of them was Huss.

[220] A little child wanted to love me, and took me in its arms, but after a while I seemed to refuse it. It signified that *we must be like children towards our Lord*. I afterwards pondered upon

this, because children have now been represented to me twice, and also in the preceding night. It means that we must not so worry about what is spiritual as to [attempt to] provide for it through our own power, nor yet for worldly things, but like a child we must cast all our cares upon our Lord.

[221] I made my way into a crowded congregation, and wanted to come out in time, but [the church] was full; nevertheless I pushed through; I came to an empty bench on which there was a cloth with which I wanted to cover myself. *It signified that I wished to come into that congregation by my own care, and that I wished to remain unknown,* as I also had done during the day; but such care should be submitted to our Lord.

[222] On awakening I had a vision, seeing much gold before me, and the air seemed to be full [of it]. *It signifies that our Lord, who disposes all things, provides for me all that I need both as to spiritual and worldly things, when like a child I cast all my care upon Him.*

[July] 22-23.

[223] It seemed as if I was taking quite a high flight, but in such a circle that I came down safely when I began to feel tired. I saw a magnificent hall with costly tapestry on the walls, all in one piece. It signified that during *the day I had kept in my mind and heart that we must allow Christ to take care for us in all that is spiritual and in all that is worldly.*

[224] I saw a boy running off with one of my shirts, and I ran after him. *This may mean that I had not washed my feet.*

[July] 24-25.

[225] Beside other things, I seemed to be in company with many persons and made merry. I seemed to be the guest of one of them. I went away thence on a journey; it appeared that I was to return, but when I went away 1 left for a journey which I had not thought of taking. I met a person who said that he had cut out a pair of bed-curtains for me, though to some extent without my knowledge. *Whether I am to take another road in*

my work and am being prepared for another [work], I know not; it is dark to me.

[July] 27-28.

[226] I saw my father in a beautiful surplice before a congregation. He spoke to me in a friendly way, and wished to take me into an inner chamber where there was a person who seemed to be asleep, and to whom he wished to tell about me. I withdrew softly, being afraid of awakening him. *This meant that I had now begun to read the Bible in the evenings, and that I was afraid that I had not properly prepared myself on Saturday evening.*

[July] 29-30.

[227] I saw a great beast which at times looked like a human being but with a great gaping mouth; he did not venture to touch me. I cut at him with a sword, but had no skill or strength in the arm to strike him. Finally I saw him standing before me with a gun from which he fired some venomous fluid; but it did not hurt me because I was protected. Immediately afterwards I thrust

the sword into his jaws, though without great force; I thrust deeper and it seemed as if it was said that he had been slain. *I had been thinking during the day about the woman and the dragon in the Apocalypse, and I wished that I might be an instrument to slay the dragon; this, however, is not within my power, but it is in the power of God alone.*

July 30-August 1.

[228] I was for a long time in holy tremors, though at the same time in deep sleep. I was wondering if I were to see something holy, and it seemed that I was thrown on my face, but I cannot affirm this for sure. Afterwards I was taken away from this [state], and behind my back I found some one with whom I seemed to be acquainted. I was vexed that he had taken me away from it, and when he went away from me I told him that he must not do so again. The tremors then continued, but further I saw nothing. *It meant that what is holy had come to me and had thus affected me, and that I was led to this work of mine which this*

day I had commenced to write: concerning the Senses; and that I wished that it would not draw me away from what is more important.

[229] Afterwards I was watching a procession of horses. There came also great, beautiful horses, of a yellowish white color, in great numbers; then more horses in beautiful pairs, which came to me; they were fat, large and beautiful, adorned with handsome harness. *This signifies the work which I have now commenced; the latter [horses] signify the work on the Brain. Thus I now perceive that I have the permission of God for this purpose, and I believe that He will give me assistance therein.*

August 4-5.

[230] I saw a person coming against me with a drawn sword. I also seemed to have a sword with a silver hilt, but when he reached me I had nothing but a broken scabbard. He lay down on my back and bit my hands. I cried for help, but there was none to be found.

[231] Postea scorto feceram As[sessore] B[renner] praesente. I seemed to boast on account

of my strength. *It signifies that I have offended against my God daily by thoughts that have clung to me, from which no human being can deliver me, but God alone; as also that I have boasted before D. [?] H. concerning my work.* I had intended the following day to go to the Lord's table, but I abstained when I perceived by means of this [the above-mentioned experience] that no man, but God alone, can grant absolution from sins. On this account it was given to me to make some observations concerning confession [before communion].

[August] 8-9.

[232] [I seemed to] arrive in Sweden and found the kingdom divided into two kingdoms; the larger one was at Upland, the other one in the direction of Orebro; there were two kings, the second being less [powerful], yet it was said his kingdom extended to Bohus[län]. I was with this one, and his kingdom increased. It appeared there was a commission for me to become secretary in Java, but I was found unfit for it as I did not know the

language; nevertheless I went. Afterwards I dreamt about some little birds which settled down about my head and which had to be picked off. *It signified that I had not properly arranged and carried out the subject of the corpus reticulare Malpighii.*

August 26-27.

[233] During the last few days I was much troubled and as it were oppressed by my sins which, it seemed to me, had not been forgiven, and which prevented me from attending the Lord's Supper the last time. Then, the last day, I seemed relieved. In the night the soles of my feet appeared altogether white, which signifies that my sins have been forgiven; and also many other things [meaning] that I was again welcome.

[August] 27-28.

[234] I seemed to take a book out of my father's library. Then I came into a ship, and was sitting with another person in the place where the rudder usually is. Yet another person was sitting at my

right hand. When I stood up, there was another person who sat down in my place, and when I wished to resume it he sat down higher up and made room for me. A woman was sittings at my left, and another one in front of me. I arose and allowed her to sit there; she sat down, but then there was no fauteuil but only an arm-chair, and I was in front of her. [235] Wine was served in large glasses and it seemed to be primrose wine; a glass was given to me which I at once emptied; it was the most delicious I have ever tasted, and without knowing what it was it occurred to me that it was heavenly nectar. The man [whom I had seen] continually sat in his place highest up by the rudder. *It signifies how I receive help in my work from a higher hand, so that I am simply used as an instrument;* on this account, moreover, I had with me a follower, whose employment, I said, was to sweep clean. This, too, signifies me.

September 1-2.

[236] I had intended to go to God's table on the second of August [September], because I had been

assured, as I had understood it, that I had been liberated from my sins, but then I beheld a large dog which ran up to me but did me no harm. I showed it to a person who stood beside me, and the dog did not hurt him either. [This signifies] *either that during the day I wanted to boast of a visit [which I had received], or else that the others around me are flattering me.*

[237] Afterwards I seemed to perceive that Didron had left his king, who had shown so much grace to him, and that he had joined the Danes, where he was slain, and that his wife, who was false to him, had caused this, and now was waiting for his body. *I now, at this very moment, heard, and it was also inspired into me, that I ought not to depart from the Church of Christ, but that I must go there to receive the Lord's Supper, and that other wise I would again become spiritually dead.* The rest I could not understand, so that there is a mystery beneath it. I kept myself away from it; I was kindled by the Holy Spirit, as is generally the case when I act according to command.

September 16th, Sunday after dinner.

[238] During the night between the fifteenth and sixteenth I beheld in my sleep two kings, the king of France and the king of Poland, and they proposed sublime things. Afterwards I saw a little girl who sang for me as I was going out: *This signified that what I had written was well-pleasing; it was the last part of the first chapter concerning the sense of touch.*

[239] Immediately after dinner, as I was sleeping there appeared to me a woman, but I did not see her face; she was rather stout and was dressed entirely in white. I wished to buy from her something to drink, but she said she had nothing left. There was a person present, however, who yielded to me his right to get a glass from her, which she had concealed in her clothes. She was, feeling for it, when I noticed how very stout she was, as if pregnant. After feeling for it in the folds of her sleeve, she found that which I was to drink. She supposed it was chocolate, but it was wine. It seemed I was not willing to take it if it was chocolate. Immediately afterwards I awoke. It

seemed to me then, as also once or twice before, that I perceived a very strong odor of wine. I wondered most at her snow-white garments. *I do not know very well what this signifies,*—whether she was the same woman *that was with me when the word "sanctuarium" was uttered, and that she now was pregnant, for I did not see her face. It may signify that I am now at work in writing correctly and give birth to that upon which I am engaged; because during that day I found myself in considerable illustration as to the matters which I had in hand.*

[September] 17-18.

[240] I saw the king of Prussia, and a person who said that he was going to cause enmity between the king of Prussia and the king of France.

[September] 18-19.

[241] I seemed to be walking across a field which was very rough. T had in my hand an iron staff which after a while was not heavy to walk

with. I came to the end of the same field, and I lay on a bed. There came against me a very large black ox and it seemed he was going to gore me with his horns. I was afraid but it was said to me: "You will get through safely." *I awoke; something will happen to me after I have finished the first chapter on the sense of touch.*

[September] 21.

[242] This was a Sunday. Before I fell asleep I was in deep thoughts concerning the things on which I am engaged in writing. Then I was told: "Hold your tongue, or I will beat you." I then saw someone sitting on a block of ice, and I was frightened. I came as it were into a vision; I held back the thoughts, and one of the usual tremors came over me. It means that I should not persist in it [my work] so long, especially on a Sunday, or perhaps in the evenings.

[September] 29-30.

[243] This was on Saturday night before Sunday. I beheld the gable-end of the most

beautiful palace that anyone could see, and the midst of it was shining like the sun. I was told that it had been resolved in the society that I was to become a member, as it were an immortal, which no one had ever been before, unless he had died and lived [again]; others said that there were several [in that state]. The thought occurred, whether it is not the most important to be with God, and thus to live. *This, therefore, had reference to that which I had just then brought to a finish concerning organic forms in general and especially the conclusion.* [244] Afterwards somebody said that he would pay me a visit at 10 o'clock, but he did not know where I lived. I replied that, as it then seemed to me, I lived in the gable-end of that palace: *which signified that the things which I then with the help of God had written concerning Forms were of such a nature that they would carry me still further, and to see things which are still more glorious.*

[245] Afterwards I was in company with women, but I was not willing to touch them, inasmuch as previously I have had to do with the

holier ones. Many things then occurred to me, which I left to the good-pleasure of God, because *I am like an instrument with which He does according to His good-pleasure, but I would wish to be with the former [holier] ones*; yet, not my will be done, but God's. God grant that I have not offended in this, which I do not believe I have done.

October 3d, in the afternoon.

[246] I was taking a little nap, when it was represented to me how everything consists inmostly of unities, the reason of the cause, the end, so that our thoughts, considered also as unities, carry within them no other end and reason than that which comes either from the spirit of God or of the body; if of the body it is all sin from the inmost, for we purpose nothing but what strives against that which is spiritual. What it is that governs us we may ourselves observe if we reflect upon our loves, which always accompany [the thoughts].

[October] 3 to 6.

[247] A number of times I have noticed that there are spirits of various kinds. The one spirit, which is the spirit of Christ, is the only one that carries all blessedness with it. By the other spirits a man is enticed in a thousand ways to follow them, but unhappy is he who does so. Once or twice there came before me Korah and Dathan, who brought strange fire to the altar and were not able to offer it. Thus it is when another fire is brought in than the one which comes from Christ. I also beheld as it were a fire that came to me. It is therefore necessary to distinguish between the spirits, which is a thing that cannot be done except through Christ Himself and His Spirit.

[248] The terrible danger in which I had been in the night between the 29th and the 30th was afterwards represented to me in the sleep; that I was upon a cake of ice which after a while could scarcely bear me; further on I came to a fearful great abyss; a person on the other side could not come to help me, and therefore I turned back. But it is God alone through Christ that has helped me

in this [peril], and He is my Lord and Master, whose slave I am. Glory be and thanks [to Him], without whom no one can come unto God.

October 6-7.

[249] I had very many and yet gracious [experiences]. There was a shining black veil or skin, which was drawn over [me], yet it had no consistency; it was said it did not hold together, and therefore it was folded up, and I was promised better enlightenment; there also appeared as it were an interior light. I wished to do it myself on Sundays. *It was that by my own understanding and imagination I had entered into something which was compared to the black veil, and which does not hold good.* Again, I saw an abyss, which means *the danger that I am in with my thoughts.* [250] Further, something was told about my book; it was said that it would be a divine Book on the worship and love of God, ["en Liber divinus de Dei cultu et amore]; I believe there was also something about spirits; I believed I had something on the subject in my work ON THE INFINITE, but there was

no reply as to that. I afterwards began to think, and received the information *that all love,—no matter for what it may be, as the love for my works on which I am now employed, if I were to love them, and not as a medium for the only love, which is the love of God and Christ Jesus,—would be a meretricious love.* On this account, also, such [love] *is always compared to whoredom in the Word of God; such also is the one that I have experienced.* But when *one has the love of God as the supreme, then one has no other love for it* [*i.e.*, one's own work] *than the one which one finds by devoting it to the service of God.* [251] I also seemed to see Czar Peter and) some other big-wigs, [knesar] who despised me because I had short sleeves; I do not know what party they were of. A number of times fine bread has been given me, and other things. May God *grant that it is, as I believe it to be, the spiritual bread.*

[252] From this and from what precedes it may be seen how quickly and easily a person may be seduced by other spirits, *who represent themselves according to the love of each one, for the loves are*

represented by spirits, and in fact as women in [the rest of the sentence is lacking].

[October] 7-8.

[253] It seemed I wanted to pass along a road, but I saw a little boy who was walking on a path; I followed him, but there was a mist. It seemed to me there were soldiers about. I walked along, crouching and afraid, but yet they did not seem to be enemies but of our own troops. But as I could not find any road before me, I turned about, and came into a room that was untidy. I asked for another chamber and also obtained it. I asked a man for some water, but he said it was stale and muddy. I then asked for milk, and woke up. *It means that I had gone astray and had followed my own understanding in a fog, and in such a case a person is afraid of his own people, as if they, were enemies. But when a person pursues the right way, then he is afraid of no one. The water means that my understanding is still turbid; the milk means that still more confirmation is required.*

[254] Afterwards, in a vision, I saw a person dressed in a black cloak, but it was taken off, and he vanished. *It means that the former blackness had vanished; when a person pursues this way only, that he puts his trust only in God and Christ, and not in himself so as to depend upon the strength of his own arm or his own understanding.* Moreover, it was perceived *that we are soldiers in order to tight against Satan continually. When one has the spirit and life of God, then there is daily a victory; but if contrariwise then there is daily a discomfiture, a falling into one defeat after another; and therefore a man should not despair but trust in the grace of God.* [255] Last night I seemed to see a commission [for me] as a Lieutenant or captain or something similar; but I asked Secretary Bierchenius to report that I desired to remain in my former office as assessor. This signified that I did not then understand what it means to be a soldier and to fight against Satan, for God sends angels along with [such a soldier] who fight for him. This is the black cloak which

was taken off, and God Himself has deigned to enlighten me.

[256] I saw also in a vision a heart full of blood, by which is meant love.

[October] 8-9.

[257] This night was the most delightful of all, because I had a vision of the Kingdom of Innocence. Beneath me I beheld the most beautiful garden that can be imagined, a garden where, little by little, white roses appeared placed upon every tree. Afterwards I came into a long chamber where beautiful white vessels were standing, containing milk and bread; it was so appetizing that nothing more appetizing can be imagined. I was in company with a woman, of whom I have no particular recollection. [258] As I returned there came to me a beautiful and innocent little child, who told me that that woman had left without saying farewell. She asked me to buy her a book which she wished to take up with her, but she did not show me. I woke up. Furthermore it seemed to me that I was giving a feast, at my own expense,

to a crowd of people in a house or palace that was standing apart. There were some acquaintances there, among others the Councillor-of-State Lagerberg, and, I believe, also Ehrenpreus and others. Everything was at my expense, and it seemed it was costing me a great deal: the thought kept coming continually that it was expensive; sometimes I did not care, for I observed that the whole expense was borne by that Lord, who owned that estate, or who showed it to me. [259] *It meant that I was in the Kingdom of Innocence and that I was giving a treat to the other and worldly; people without seeing them; perhaps it signifies my work, that it should not he like them, although I am giving them a treat by it, or something else. The child meant innocence itself; I was quite touched by it, and wished that I were in such a kingdom, where all is innocence. I lamented that I had to leave it, upon awakening. As to the woman who left without sayings farewell, I do not know what is meant thereby.*

[260] On the next day, the 9th, my eyesight was so strong that I was able to read the small-print Bible without the least inconvenience.

[October] 9-10.

[261] In a vision there appeared as it were a fire of hard coal, burning briskly; it signified ignem amoris. Postea cum foemina eram cui dentes quoddam in loco quod attingere volebam sed dentes obstabant.

It signified that during the day I had been engaged upon my *work, which is entirely different front the other one and* [proceeds from] *an entrely different love.* [I was in doubt] *whether it would prevail, and whether it would not be regarded as mere talk or a plaything in comparison with the other one.* [262] *Upon awakening I had fully resolved* to abandon this work; this also I would I have done, if it had not afterwards seemed to me in my sleep that I had been sent to a certain place with a letter. I did not find the way, but my sister, Hedwig, saw the letter, and said that it was addressed to Ulrika Adlersteen, who, it appeared, had longed for me for a long time. I arrived there, and also saw Schönström. Afterwards I had continually before me the thought of the senses, how they ascend to the brain and again descend, *by which I was strengthened to continue with the work.* [263] *May God grant that this may not be contrary to His good-pleasure, since I cannot take anything from the sleep without getting myself into a temptation to abandon it. God, however, helped me to this resolution* [to continue with the work]. *To God alone be praise and honor.* Nevertheless, a child stumbled over my foot, hurt itself, and screamed. I wanted to help it up and asked. Why do you race about so? *It meant, without doubt, that I wanted to hurry too fast in this* [work].

[October] 10-11.

[264] Videbar mihi sicut in lecto esse una cum foemina, sed earn non tetigi.

I then met a gentleman whom I asked if I could enter his service, because I had lost my fortune on account of the war, but the answer was, No. They seemed to be playing basset; the money kept changing hands, but I was with them all the time. I asked my man-servant if he had said that I owned anything; he answered that he had not, and I said that he should not say anything but this. *It signifies the Moravian Church, that I am there and am not accepted, and that I say that I have no knowledge in religion but have lost it all; and that those who play basset, win now and then.*

[October] 12-13.

[265] It seemed as if someone was being beaten and scourged, and afterwards he preached with greater zeal and insisted upon it both [in the pulpit] above and [on the floor] below. *It signifies that when a person has been chastised by our Lord, he will afterwards get greater zeal and spirit to persist in that to which the spirit leads him, so that chastisement and punishment give increase in it. I was wondering, yesterday, when I was so happy and allowed my thoughts to run somewhat freely, whether punishment would change it, whereupon this came as an answer.*

[266] Afterwards I seemed to say to myself that the Lord Himself will instruct me; *for I found that I am in such a condition that I know nothing about it [religion] except that Christ must be the all in all, or God through Christ, so that we ourselves are not able to do the least thing towards it, and still less strive for it; and therefore it is best to surrender oneself unconditionally; and, further, that if one could be entirely passive in this thing, it would be the most perfect [state].* [267] I saw also in a vision that beautiful loaves of bread were presented to me on a plate. *This was a premonition that the Lord Himself will instruct me, since I have now first come into such a state that I know nothing, and that all preconceived opinions have been taken away from me, which is the beginning of learning, viz., that one must first become a child, and then be wet-nursed into knowledge, as is now taking place with me.*

[October] 13-14.

[268] Among other things it was said to me that since the last fortnight I had begun to look much

more handsome, and to be like an angel. *God grant that this be so! May God stand by me in this and not take His grace away from me.*

[October] 15-16.

[269] In a *vision* there appeared a person who was carrying a heavy burden, and he was carrying wooden planks; he fell down under the burden, and another person came to help him, but in what manner he was helped up I did not see. In *the sleep* it appeared after a while that I was walking across on a board, and that I was seeing an abyss and perils before me; afterwards I climbed up a rope after another person, but did not see the top or how I might reach it. *It signifies that those who of their own selves strive to help themselves into the kingdom of heaven, or to that which is higher, labor in vain, and are in constant peril: but it is easy when a person addresses himself to God, who is the help in such and* ———

October 18-19.

[270] I dreamt that a big dog, which I supposed was tied, flew at me and bit me in the leg; someone came and held his terrible jaws so that he could do no more evil. *It meant that yesterday I had listened to an oration at the College of Medicine, and was so presumptuous in my thoughts as to imagine that they might mention me as one who was somewhat prominent in the understanding of anatomy; yet I was glad that it was not done.* During the night following it appeared to me in a vision as if someone with a twisted foot had left me, which *may mean that on account of the dog's bite I had become like one with a twisted foot.*

[October] 19-20.

[271] I dreamt that I saw one beast after another, which spread out their wings; they were dragons. I flew away above them, yet one of them I struck against. *Such dragons signify spurious loves, which show themselves as if they were not*

dragons, before their wings are seen. It was on this subject that I was then writing.

[October] 20-21.

[272] *It was very gracious and wonderful: during the preceding day I had found myself unworthy of all the grace which God has deigned to show to me, because with me the love of self and the pride were so deeply rooted. I therefore prayed to God to take this away from me, since it is not within my own power. In the evening I found myself in a strange situation, such as I had never before experienced, viz., that I, as it were, despaired of the grace of God, even though I knew that God is so gracious, and that He has shown to me especially a greater grace than to others. It was an anxiety in the soul, but not in the mind, so that it could not be felt except in the mind itself, without any pain in the body.* [273] I fell asleep again, and there appeared two dogs which followed me closely; after a long while I got rid of them, and it was said to me in my thoughts that this strange pain was to cure me of them. *There is such a pain,*

therefore, when the root is to be removed from that which is so deeply rooted; this is well worth remembering and keeping in the thoughts.

[274] Afterwards I saw a great king; it was the King of France, who went about without a suite and in such lowly estate that he could not from it be recognized as a king. There was one with me who did not seem willing to acknowledge him as king, but I said that he is of such a character as to care nothing for it. He was very courteous towards all, without distinction, and spoke also with me. As he left he was still without a suite and took upon himself the burdens of other persons, and carried as it were a load of clothes; but later he came into a very different company, where there was much more magnificent estate. [275] Afterwards I saw the Queen; a chamberlain then came and bowed before her, and she also made just as deep a reverence, and there was nothing of pride in her. *It signifies that in Christ there is not the least degree of pride, but He makes Himself the equal of others; and although He is the greatest of Kings, He cares nothing for grandeur, and He also*

takes the burdens of others upon Himself. The Queen, who is Wisdom, is of the same nature: she has no love of self, and does not regard herself as more lofty because she is Queen.

October 26-27.

[276] *I had been foretold that the 27th of October would return; it was when I undertook the* WORSHIP AND LOVE OF GOD. It seemed as if it were Christ Himself, with whom I associated as with another person, without ceremony. He borrowed a little money from another person, about five pounds. I was vexed because He did not borrow from me. I took up two [pounds], but it seemed to me that I dropped one of them, and likewise the other one. He asked what it was. I said that I had found two, and that one of them might have been dropped by Him. I handed them over, and He accepted. In such an innocent manner we seemed to live together, which was a state of innocence.

[277] Afterwards I was in my chamber together with some other acquaintance or relative, and I said that I wished to show him that I had better

lodgings, I therefore went out with him first into an adjoining chamber, which extended far away, and chamber after chamber, but they did not belong to me. Someone in a bed asked what was wanted. I went out with him into my own parlor; when I opened the door I saw that a whole market-place was lodged there; right in front of me there was a great deal of merchandise, and beyond it there appeared the flank of a great palace, but this was taken down. Then, in front and at the sides, everything appeared full of beautiful vessels, porcelain, as it seemed to me, and as if recently arranged there; on the side everything was still being arranged. Afterwards I went into my own little chamber, which also was shining. [278] *This signifies the whole of that work upon which I am now entering in the name of God; in front, before me, is the [part] concerning the Worship of God, at the sides [the part] concerning the Love; and also that I ought not to take from the wares of others, but my own, as it was in my parlor which I hired, my chamber, and besides it was the other work, and the rooms at the side meant that which did not belong to me. May God lead me in the right way!* Christ said that I ought not to undertake anything without Him.

[279] I mounted a fine black horse; there were two; he was frisky; at first he went out of the way, but afterwards he turned back. It meant that which I should undertake, which still was dark to me, but after a while it will come in the right way.

[280] While I was going with my friend through a long passage there came a beautiful girl; she fell into his arms and moaned. I asked her if she knew him, but she did not answer. I took her away from him and led her by the arm. This was my other work to which she addressed elf, and from which I took her away thus.

[281] In the morning there appeared to me in a vision a market like the "Disting" fair; it was in my father's house at Upsala, in the parlor upstairs, in the entrance, and all over the house. *This signifies the same [as above], so that it must be done all the more surely.*

[282] In the morning when I awoke, there came again upon me such a swoon or fainting fit as I

experienced six or seven years ago in Amsterdam, when I entered upon the Economy of THE ANIMAL KINGDOM, but it was much more subtle, so that I seemed near to death; it came upon me as I saw daylight and it threw me on my face; gradually, however, it passed off because I fell into brief slumbers. This swoon, therefore, was more internal and deeper, but passed off right away. *This signifies, as at the former time, that my head is being put in order and is actually being cleansed of all that which might obstruct these thoughts, as also happened at the former time, because it gave me penetration, especially with the pen,* as now also was represented to me in that I seemed to be writing a fine hand.

[The last four words of the preceding sentence are written on the 99th page of the original manuscript, but the rest of the page is blank. After several blank pages the following memoranda are found:]

[283] Videbar mihi cum Oehlrich foeminisque duabus esse. Cubuit, et dein, ut videtur, erat cum foeminarum una quam detexit. Mihi occurrit, ut dixi, quod et ego illarum unæ accubuissem, quodque pater meus id vidisset, sed præterivit, de hac re ne quidem verbum dicens.

[284] I left Oelreich. On the way there was deep water, but at the side there was a passage where there was very little water. I therefore went thither along the side, for I thought I ought not to walk in the deep water.

[285]—It seemed as if a sky-rocket burst above me, shedding a mass of sparks of beautiful fire. It means, perhaps, love for what is high.

[On another blank page, at the end of the original manuscript, Swedenborg gives the following explanation, in Latin, of a statement made in n. 213, as follows:]

[286] Verities or virgins of this kind regard it as shameful to offer themselves for sale; they esteem themselves so precious and dear to their admirers

that they show indignation if anyone offers a price, and still more if anyone attempts to purchase them; to others, who hold them vile, they lift their eyebrows.

And therefore, lest by the former they should be held beneath valuation, and fall into contempt with the latter, they would rather offer themselves freely to their lovers. I, who am their servitor, would not dare but to obey them, lest I be deprived of the service.

THE END.

Printed in Great Britain
by Amazon